# ULTIMATE PLEASURE

## THE SECRETS OF
## EASILY ORGASMIC WOMEN

# ULTIMATE PLEASURE

## THE SECRETS OF
## EASILY ORGASMIC WOMEN

# Marc and Judith Meshorer

ST. MARTIN'S PRESS
NEW YORK

Design by Amy Bernstein

Library of Congress Cataloging in Publication Data

Meshorer, Marc.
    Ultimate pleasure.

    1. Orgasm, Female.   2. Women—Sexual behavior.
I. Meshorer, Judith.   II. Title.
HQ29.M47   1986          155.3'4          86-3979
ISBN 0-312-82826-8

To the memory of
Birdie Ascherman Meshorer
and
Abraham H. Maslow

# CONTENTS

# ACKNOWLEDGMENTS

We are grateful to Heide Lange, our literary agent, for her warmth, faith, and always-expert assistance. Thanks, Heide. You made the diference.

Joyce Engelson saw promise, acquired the manuscript in progress, and helped shape the final work for the pleasure of general readers. Victoria Skurnick and Robin Desser, our editors, devoted care and extra hours toward bringing the book to fruition.

Catherine Shaw worked with us throughout the initial writing of this book; her sensitivity and editing skills are everywhere present in the manuscript. Beth Kennard researched the professional literature; Heather Broadhurst analyzed research data and entered it into the computer.

Irving Rosen, M.D., Ruth Rosen, A.C.S.W., and Maureve Goldhamer, M.A., helped us from the beginning, read while the writing was in progress, and gave us insightful suggestions. We are also grateful to the following health professionals who read the book at various stages, and who gave us encouragement and comment: Irwin Moore, M.D.; Chester L. Plotkin, M.D.; Marcia E. Aron, R.N., M.S., and Jack D. Aron, M.D.; Ilze K. Schwartz, M.D., and Richard A. Schwartz, M.D.; Howard A. Hoffman, M.D.; Claire Foudraine, R.N.; Raphael S. Good, M.D.; Nancy K. Johnson, M.D.; Stella Resnick, Ph.D.; Ellen Frank, Ph.D.; and Ronald S. Immerman, M.D.

Patricia Worth, always empathetic and supportive, was our principal co-interviewer. Karen Rastatter, Terry Luria, Beryl Moore, Diane Horton Modzelewski, and Lora Thompson were all valued co-interviewers.

And finally, appreciatively, we acknowledge the contribution of the women who participated in this study. They gave of their most private selves. This book is a gift, from them.

# FOREWORD BY BEVERLY WHIPPLE, PH.D.

*Ultimate Pleasure* is a book about easily orgasmic women. It is both a "how-to" and a "self-help" book, which tells how easily orgasmic women obtain pleasure. Since my own values emphasize pleasure-oriented sexual interactions rather than goal-oriented sexual interactions, I was at first concerned that *Ultimate Pleasure* would be goal-oriented and not pleasure-oriented. I was concerned that it would focus on orgasm as an end in itself, and not stress the pleasures that can be enjoyed from sexual interactions with or without orgasms. But, as Marc and Judith Meshorer point out in Chapter 2, orgasm is not a goal in itself, and striving for it is usually self-defeating and not pleasurable.

My concern whenever I speak or write about female sexual response, or on the research I have done in this area, is that I do not want to create new pressures for women or men. I hope that by disseminating new information, it will help to validate the experiences of many, provide new options for some, and help stimulate open communication between partners.

We are all sexual beings from the day we are born until the day we die. We have the choice of expressing our sexuality in many ways. Sometimes holding someone's hand or being held is a completely fulfilling experience and does not have to lead into any further sexual involvement. Orgasm does not have to be the inevitable goal. The pleasure one receives from holding hands, being held, oral sex, self-stimulation, or any other form of stimulation can be enjoyed as an end in itself, and does not necessarily have to lead to any other sexual activity.

Although the Meshorers and I view differently the importance of some issues in this book, the areas in which we differ do not override the basic concept—upon which we fully agree —that women are unique sexual beings who can take responsibility for their own sexual response. Because each woman responds uniquely to sexual stimulation and pleasurable experiences, it is important for every woman to be aware of what she finds pleasurable and to acknowledge this to herself, and then to communicate all of this to her partner. Women often have to give themselves permission to enjoy what they find pleasurable. We live in a society that finds little value and few words for pleasure, but much value and more than two hundred words for pain. We have much to overcome and learn, and this book, *Ultimate Pleasure,* helps us to appreciate the value of pleasure. It helps each woman to realize that her unique sexual response falls within the wide range of normal, and it provides suggestions for both men and women to enhance sexual pleasure.

# INTRODUCTION

We have sought the knowledge of experts—women who are, themselves, easily orgasmic during lovemaking with a partner. All agreed to participate within the following context: "A dear friend or close sister asks your help. . . . She has a reasonably desirable partner but has difficulty achieving orgasm. What detailed and specific advice can you give her?"

We interviewed a broad cross section of primarily heterosexual American women. Of the sixty participants, half are married and living with their husbands, two were married but had separated, one is widowed, fifteen are divorced, and twelve have never married. Among the married women, length of marriage ranged from two months to thirty-four years.

The average age of the women is 32.35 years, with a range from 21 to 59.

Women were also selected on the basis of family religious background. Thirty women (50 percent) are from Protestant backgrounds, eighteen (30 percent) Catholic, and twelve (20 percent) Jewish.

Racially, fifty-four women are Caucasian and six are black.

Eight women hold graduate-school degrees; two did not graduate from high school. The average woman in the study has completed a year or two of college; many are continuing their education.

Occupations are also quite varied. Eight women are health professionals (therapists, social workers, nurses), and eight are in creative fields (artists, performers, media communicators). Two are factory workers, four are students, seven are teachers, nine are homemakers, and twenty-two are businesswomen working in management, sales, administrative, or clerical capacities. While the average woman might be characterized as "middle class," the range is broad, from the lower to upper fringes of middle, with the latter group represented by women of substantial education, social status, and affluence.

Thirty-five of the women have given birth to children, the maximum number being six.

Although we will occasionally use "averages" to describe these women, they are, as a group, anything but average or randomly chosen. First, the basis of participation was that they be "easily orgasmic." Second, women who volunteer for a study such as this are, by necessity, different from women whose modesty and reserve would make participation impossible.

From one to four weeks in advance of the interview, participants completed the questionnaire contained in Appendix B. Privacy was assured; therefore the names appearing in this book are names assigned by the authors.

All interviews were conducted by a male/female co-interview team, and the interview atmosphere was extremely informal.

For more information on research methods, please refer to Appendix A.

The basic criterion for inclusion in the study was that a woman be easily orgasmic in heterosexual contacts with a partner. "Easily orgasmic" was arbitrarily defined as being able to reach orgasm during *at least* 75 percent of sexual contacts, and describes consistency or reliability in reaching orgasm, not rapidity. We followed a criterion that simply required obtaining orgasm during a sexual contact or episode with a partner, whether through intercourse alone, intercourse assisted by other stimulation, through other stimulations alone—or by any combinations.

We provide the following numerical descriptions as a means of verifying the participants' rightful place in this group.

The "average woman" in this study is orgasmic in over 90 percent of her sexual contacts with a partner.

During a normal or usual sexual contact, she obtains an average of three orgasms. This average, however, is exaggerated upward by a handful of women who are extremely orgasmic. The median number of orgasms—the number usually experienced by women in the middle ranks of the group—is a more meaningful description, in this instance, two.

During their most orgasmic encounters, the women average nine orgasms. Again, a median is more meaningful here, the number being four.

The average woman has three sexual encounters per week. Among single and divorced women particularly, this number is notably variable.

The average woman is orgasmic from three distinct types of triggering stimulation: usually coital, manual, and oral. One woman, at the upper end of the range, is orgasmic from nine different types of triggering stimulation.

Of sixty women, forty-four often experience some form of multiple orgasm, five occasionally do, seven rarely do, and four never do.

Four women are extremely orgasmic—they achieve six to a dozen orgasms in their average encounters; two of these women report an upper range of one hundred. We have termed these women "ultra orgasmic," and will discuss them in the chapter on multiple orgasm.

Ultimately, numbers mean nothing. They are never an index of sexual satisfaction, nor a measure of the quality of a relationship. It is, moreover, our subjective but firm impression that as much *sexual* energy can be expended in *one* orgasm as in a hundred, and as much personal, emotional, and spiritual pleasure derived from *one* as from a thousand. As Bernadette, an ex-nun, said, "When I'm coming, when I'm having a real good orgasm, I feel spiritual, I'm just not here, I'm in heaven. The most exciting form of being alive is enjoying the sexual act. That's when you're most like God."

Finally, let us remember: Being orgasmic with partners is not the total substance of female sexuality. Moments of communion, of quiet bliss, transcendence, may sometimes supersede a woman's desire for orgasm. Further, she may not be orgasmic *at all,* yet fully share the delights of making love with another.

She—and her partner—must not feel pressure "to perform." Being orgasmic is simply a choice that a woman may wish to have.

One of the authors did graduate work with Abraham H. Maslow, an eminent psychologist who stressed research from the viewpoint of human health and growth. We view our research, and this book, as greatly Maslovian in spirit. Exploratory, based on robust sexual health, and told through the women's own voices, it adds a new dimension to our step-by-step understanding of how a woman, in actual life, obtains orgasmic pleasure.

For the average woman you will meet, however, two years elapsed between her first intercourse and becoming easily orgasmic during lovemaking with a partner. Yet, if a woman is sexually active, it surely need not take that long. Many women expressed the hope that by sharing their intimate knowledge, less orgasmic women would save time and heartache—and that very orgasmic women would renew or expand their pleasure.

To be orgasmic when making love, *all* women, of course, need a considerate partner; male readers will benefit at least as much as women.

In the major portion of this book, the women describe how they obtain ultimate pleasure, their orgasm. We learn how orgasmic women prepare themselves for lovemaking, how they focus in and eliminate distraction, how they build sensation. We sense a steady progression as a woman approaches her climax, an integration of body and mind, a quest for enhanced stimulation, a celebration of joy . . . but we're leaping ahead of our story!

First we will offer a glimpse of the lives of orgasmic women, then move on to the central delight—learning how these women make love, and how they help assure that they will be orgasmic with partners.

# ULTIMATE PLEASURE

## THE SECRETS OF
## EASILY ORGASMIC WOMEN

# Becoming Orgasmic With Partners

*I don't depend on my husband to give me orgasms. It's a shared experience.*

*—Tracy*

*Zarek was very special. He taught me about the pleasures I was keeping from myself.*

*—Wendy*

Before a woman can integrate sex within a stable relationship, she needs to gain some knowledge—about herself, her needs and skills, the nature of sex with a lover.

Her learning begins with herself. Natalie, a mother in her early thirties, is a petite, attractive woman with long auburn hair and expressive blue eyes. Now and then she leans forward as she tells of past emotions, as if to be sure we understand the meaning of her story.

The earliest sexual feelings Natalie remembers stemmed from an incident at about the age of seven, when, toweling dry after a bath, she experienced a potent orgasm: "That first made a big imprint on my mind. I had no idea what it was. I was frightened. It felt great—but I must have felt all kinds of guilt. It freaked me out. So, I think I felt a feeling, got dressed, and ignored it . . . for years and years. I never masturbated again until late in my marriage, and I was convinced that anybody who did was totally looney-tunes.

"My mother and I had a typical Jewish mother-daughter relationship, a lot of conflicts. But she had a problem separating from me, allowing me to be mature and adult, and I guess I had a problem separating from her. She felt me an extension of herself.

"Growing up, the general feeling I had about sex was that

your body was very much hidden. My mother talked about it occasionally, but I was afraid to ask questions, and I never got the feeling that sex was okay. I *did* get the feeling you wait until you're married."

Through her teens Natalie slowly progressed to petting with her clothes off and consciously going for orgasm by "dry humping," rubbing her clitoral area on a boyfriend's leg or torso. She remained a virgin—until a week after leaving home for college: "He was older. He was Gentile. He lived out of town. He was everything my mother was not! The setting was very romantic. We were on the ocean, in a cottage, and I felt myself filling up with all this unbelievable passion that I had never felt before. I had very pretty lingerie—we weren't hippies yet, we were going to be hippies in another couple of months—and we walked the beach and came back to the cottage, had wine and cheese, and proceeded to make love on the couch. Except I had my period and my Tampax was still in! I was afraid to tell him, afraid to take the Tampax out and offend him or spoil the mood. Oral sex brought me to an orgasm—I'd never had oral sex before. I was aroused. I mean when he went down on me, I doubt if I thought 'What about the string?' or 'Is this the way it's supposed to be?' I figured the hell with it. If he didn't care, I didn't care. Then he went inside me, Tampax and all, and I thought, 'This is what I've been waiting all my life for?'

"He was great and it was nice, but it was missing something —missing a lot of things. After the weekend I did nothing but shower my sins away. I felt tremendous guilt and ambivalence, like, 'Wait a minute, this is such a nice feeling, why shouldn't I feel this?', then 'No, no, no, it's not right,' and 'Yes, yes, you only have one life to live.' But I became fairly promiscuous. Guess I also felt—I think I'd heard that—you do it once, why not do it a hundred times? So I did it a hundred times."

Although "missing something," Natalie enjoyed a varied and orgasmic sex life—until she returned to her hometown and married. "When I got married, I turned off, repressed all I had learned or thought I'd learned. I told myself, 'Well, I want the wedding. I want the showers and I want the clothes and I want the honeymoon. I want the little apartment. I want the little kitchen. And I want . . . ' Well, all those things that I thought came next." Communication with David, her new husband, was stifled: "He was afraid to tell me what he enjoyed because he also came from a Jewish family and he felt that you marry a nice Jewish girl but you certainly don't fuck her." Also, she had yet to break free of her mother: "I remember the experience of feeling that my mother, psychologically, was standing over the bed—and if she wasn't there, she was waiting in the bathroom!"

As Natalie's sexual interest declined, her self-image worsened. While pregnant in her late twenties, she gained an enormous amount of weight: "The first year after her birth was hell. The last thing I wanted was to fuck. I felt like a piece of putty, certainly not like a person, except for my breasts, because I was nursing and supplying this child with nutrition. The rest of me didn't exist."

That was rock bottom.

Rescue began with herself. She started by losing weight. "Then I found sensations through nursing, sensations I had read about and started to feel free about. I became friendly with other women and verbalized my sexuality. I found that some of them actually masturbated, and I felt free to ask why and how, to tell them I never had done so. One day, some two years after my child was born, I was home taking a shower. I had lost fifty pounds and had started to feel like a person again. All of a sudden my body felt different, great, and sensation came over me. I got out of the shower and on my bed, touched myself on the clitoris—and got off with an orgasm. Right after, I remember feeling relieved and free, feeling *a freedom from my mother.* I felt that I had finally achieved this wonderful thing by myself, without having to go to her for help, totally on my own."

This experience helped Natalie open communication; she

discovered that David was a sympathetic partner who "wanted us to grow." Today she feels their relationship is exciting, fulfilling, and solid.

Looking back, Natalie muses: "I didn't feel that I had any control over what my body was doing or saying or feeling, and didn't allow my body to feel doors,* or breasts, or clitoris. My vagina was so tight, my ass was so tight—I mean nothing opened to anything. I wasn't willing to hold and keep my own sexual identity."

Fathers, too, play a crucial role in a woman's sexual development. There is evidence that low-orgasmic women, in addition to having concerns about closeness with their mothers, are preoccupied with feelings that their fathers are unavailable for a substantial or consistent relationship. A distant father is already half lost; his growing daughter may interpret his apparent uncaringness and unreliability as meaning she's bad and unworthy. Enjoying sexual feelings, by herself or with another, might make her doubly "bad" and risk the loss of her father's love—or that of her partners thereafter.

Many of these issues are echoed in Vivian's experience. She is a small, physically active woman of fifty years, carefully groomed and refined in appearance. From a Protestant background, she is twice divorced and the mother of four children, all from her first marriage. Vivian's first intercourse was at the age of thirteen, her first orgasm was at eighteen, but she did not become consistently orgasmic with a partner until four years ago—twenty-eight years after her first orgasm with a partner.

Daughters are often prey to a mother's sexual anxieties. Vivian remembers: "When I was growing up, my mother's whole idea was if I ever did anything wrong, she would cry. I'll

---

*This is a reference to the vaginal doors of Natalie's orgasmic image, described in Chapter 9.

never forget that. Instead of telling me what it would do to *me,* all she ever told me is what it would do to *her.*

"I think my desire for closeness to a man has something to do with my dad. He's still around and I think the world of him, but we were never close. He's hard to touch and he kind of kept his distance. If I kiss him, today, it's rare, and he greeted me the other day with a big hug and I couldn't believe it—it's just not him. I think the lack of attention from a man in my home, from my father maybe, was why I was looking for attention from men while I was growing up, but as far as being sexually satisfied—I never was."

During her marriages, Vivian found her sexual desires a source of guilt as well as pleasure. "If I had an orgasm, I didn't know what brought it on, and I had no idea how to make it happen again—I just didn't know that much about myself. But I always did feel sexual, and I always felt guilty that I wanted more sex. I connected wanting a lot of sex with a woman who was a whore or something—a normal, average woman doesn't have that kind of desire. And don't be afraid of masturbation —it took me so long to realize that it's not such a terrible thing after all. What's wrong with it? Why shouldn't you understand your own body? But the guilt I had all those years. . . ."

Sometimes a helpful partner encourages a woman's readiness to explore her sexuality. After her second divorce, children grown and independent, Vivian found two such partners. The first was a man ten years younger. The second, her current lover, is all the more appreciative of her vital sensuality, perhaps because of severe restraints in his long former marriage.

"He took such an interest in satisfying a woman when I came along, and I was very willing to learn—just a good combination. Communication was number one, telling him what I wanted. I couldn't do it when we first met. I said, 'I don't want to tell you. If you don't know what to do, forget it. That spoils it.' But as we made love he'd say, 'Is this what you like? You've got to tell me.' Or 'Am I doing the right thing?' And he got me to open up more and more. I still have a little trouble with it, but there's nothing more important than letting your guy know what you like and what you want—he likes to hear it, to know he's doing the right thing. I could have done that before if I'd known, with either husband, and I think we'd have had a lot better sex life—oh boy, do I ever. So many women don't understand themselves, blame their frustrations on somebody else, and it doesn't have to be that way.

"I always have orgasms now—even when he merely suggests that I should, or kisses my neck, or the small of my back. . . . There's nothing like it. When we're making love, I'm young again. . . . I'm ageless at a time like that."

## Becoming Independent

During adolescence, a young woman consciously seeks her personal sexual identity. She begins to feel separate from her parents, and adolescent conflicts, however unpleasant, assist her separation. Ideally, this exploration and testing leads to high self-esteem and an independent identity, yet none of this happens with clockwork precision or robotlike uniformity.

Iris first had intercourse at twelve, the earliest of the women in our study. She is an executive secretary, age twenty-one, the youngest of three sisters, and was raised as a Presbyterian. Small, almost frail, she still conveys an impression of saucy strength and vitality.

"I had a very young period, at nine and a half or ten years of age, before my mother or school told me anything. I first kissed a boy when I was about ten. When I was nine or ten, I imagined making love with a girl. When I was eleven, a girl of fourteen took me to her bedroom to talk about periods. She showed me her pubic hair, spread her legs, and got me into a little petting.

"I was a wild, 'bad' girl in junior high, infatuated with my girlfriend's older brother. I was twelve, he was about seventeen, and I had the idea in mind, but it was his doing. After we had intercourse, I sort of felt indifferent: 'What's the big deal?' At fifteen I met my first real lover, a man who was thirty-three. I was attracted to him—he hung around where I shot pool—and I decided this was my chance; he had his own apartment, and I was *ready*. I never backed away: I had orgasms from oral sex and intercourse the first time we made love. I was with him for a year and a half, and he was great at making love—aggressive, dominant but tender, and later, with him, I was all these myself. I can't count the men—or women—after him, but I'm usually orgasmic with both.

"I graduated high school, but I've been working since I was fifteen, earning my own money and clothes. I remember when I was seventeen I wanted to visit a boyfriend in Florida, and my father threatened to kick me out of the house. I had no idea if he would, but I had plenty of places to stay at the time, so that was the least of my problems. Having jobs helped me a lot. I bought what I wanted for myself—it wasn't like Mother picked out my shoes—and I also figured I could run my own body...."

Few of the women in this study rebelled as audaciously as Iris. The great majority, avoiding severe confrontations with their parents, made "time-appropriate" decisions for personal and sexual freedom. One woman relates:

I guess I know how it happened. I asked my mother to
provide transportation back to school after my
appointment with a gynecologist for birth-control pills.
She was looking for an explanation, and I gave her
one. She told me that she had consulted her doctor
about when I should see a gyn, and he had supposedly
said, "When she gets married." I told her I thought it
was *before* I got married, and sort of let her know that
I had decided on my own way of doing things.

Often the decision is gradual, as another woman explains:

> Eventually it came down to the "Big It"—you know,
> "Did you do it?" I had always planned on saving it,
> but I gradually decided differently. Still, I don't think I
> ever consciously thought about whether I would or
> wouldn't before I did.

Or, the decision is made with a fiancé, or within the bounds of marriage:

> I was a "good girl" until I met my future husband; if
> *he* said "okay," it was okay.

> My parents never talked about sex, but just before I
> was married my mother told me, "If you can't make
> your husband happy in bed, there's no marriage." I
> had an orgasm with my first intercourse and thought it
> was *terrific!*

When parents communicated positive attitudes about sexuality and also encouraged their daughters' independence, the women became easily orgasmic *twice as quickly* as the women in the total group.

Tracy is in her late twenties, from a conservative Jewish background. A lissome woman with light brown hair, she moves with buoyant, athletic grace, and her manner is open and cheerful:

"There was lots of affection in our house, kissing and hugging and touching various parts of the body—I knew my parents had a sexual relationship. Having an older brother and sister really broke the ice for me. When my brother wasn't married, I knew that lady friends would sleep over on occasion, and he would have boy-girl parties on the back porch—which they called Bun Hill. The parties were never rowdy, but I'd wake up in the morning and there would be bodies sacked out all over the place, even though my folks were home and totally aware. That's how my parents raised us, thank God—we were free spirits.

"My folks always knew what was happening and I never hid anything from them. If I was going to stay out overnight, I would simply call and let them know that I wasn't coming home. But we all made excellent grades—both my brothers are scientists—and we were all independent."

Tracy enjoyed sex from a fairly early age: "My body was capable of vaginal lubrication from petting when I was still pretty young, but it bothered me at first because I didn't know what it was. At about fourteen I discovered masturbation. It felt really good, but it took two years to learn how my body responded. You see, I didn't know what I was looking for.

"When we made out in those days, we did almost everything —it was like having intercourse with your clothes on, dry humping. It was kissing, it was hugging, it was 'Did you score?', it was copping a feel—that's my generation and I liked it.

"I had intercourse when I was sixteen. I had dated the boy a few times; he was adorable and petite, and I wanted to share my body with the right person. It was a 'feeling' thing—I had decided that if the person was right, the time was right, and it felt right, I would do it.

"We were at a party but wanted to be alone, and went to a bathhouse behind the pool. We were kissing and touching and hugging, and I was just so hot I felt like ripping his clothes off and doing it. I was completely open with him, told him that I had never had intercourse, and he was open with me, and very understanding. Eventually we took each other's clothes off, and it was just a progression from top to bottom. I asked him to explain things as he went along, and he told me what he was going to do. I was extremely comfortable and relaxed, calm. And for some reason, I didn't bleed, even though I lost my virginity that night.

"It was a very pleasurable experience. I did not feel any guilt. In fact, it made me feel free that I had done this, and then I felt more of a woman, more of a whole person. And it was beautiful —the fact that I had shared this experience with someone."

Soon after, this young man left the country for schooling abroad, and Tracy experienced her first orgasm with another partner, through oral sex: "It was marvelous!"

Tracy left home for college, worked in California for several years, and enjoyed a variety of partners over the ten-year span before she married. "With each of the people that I got intimate with, if something wasn't happening, I would always know what worked. I could always get off on fingering, or what the other person was like, or oral sex could always do it—there was always a little ace in the hole. But since I've gotten married, the love that I share with my husband is so beautiful, I'm so in love with him and he's so in love with me, that he just touches and kisses me, and I come."

Naturally, whatever parental attitudes may be, the woman herself has the final say as to when she becomes independent— and whether she will be orgasmic.

Grace is a nursing administrator, working on her masters in medical technology. She currently lives in a luxurious home and is married to a prominent cardiologist. In her early thirties, the fifth of ten children from an Eastern-seaboard, old-line Catholic family, she pats back wisps of her long blond hair in a way that suggests "proper" breeding, and quietly reminisces:

"I wasn't close to my older sister and no one talked about sex. I thought you could get pregnant from French kissing. My father was almost abusive, and Mother was *repulsed* by sex— she thought that men were animals, and constantly downgraded our father. I was never allowed to date or pick my own clothes. My parents tried to control and isolate me, even when I went to a Catholic nursing college, close to where we lived. They insisted I live in a single room, and I had to go home every weekend."

However, even the most controlling parents can lose their hold on a daughter: "I talked with the girls at nursing college and learned a lot about sex. The girls taught me how to dress and put on makeup, and I learned about bodies in my classes. And I was nervy; the other girls would go to parties with medical students and fraternities, where they served ethyl alcohol for liquor. I would help snitch it from the labs for them, though I had never been allowed to drink. One weekend—I was always supposed to be home by six o'clock on Friday—I went to a fraternity party instead, and sat there drinking ethyl. I was having a *wonderful* time—until I tried to stand up and dance!

"Someone took me home; my mother was waiting, threatening to thrash me. I talked back—'Don't strike me!' I said. Well, my father, thank God, had come in behind me, saw what condition I was in, just shook his head and said, 'I think she needs to be left alone.' My mother had wanted to carry on further, and my father just told her, *'Sit down.'* He took me upstairs, sat me on the bed, and said, 'If you're going to drink, you've got to learn some things.' He told me how to handle headaches, and said you could get to being smashed and lose control of behavior. And he asked me, 'Did your mother ever discuss sex life with you?' I was really feeling good and I said to him, 'No, but I did read a book about a hundred and one ways to do it!' I remember his reaction. He covered his face like this, and he brought his hands down, and he had this grin and he said, 'That's okay, honey, I think you'll be okay.'

"The next day he sent my sisters to continue my education. We started talking about the night before and they asked me what I had done. My sister said, 'What was Mom's face like?' and that told me they didn't accept her either. I realized if I were to go against my mother, I would not lose my family's support."

The next week, with additional support from her college's Mother Superior and another nun, she wrote her parents a letter demanding the freedom to date. Her father gave permission, a turning point. "I changed. I realized I had guts."

Grace became a political activist, a demonstrator, the president of a national student organization, a feminist, a "hard-assed radical"—and eventually ran into enough mischief and controversy to get her, temporarily, expelled from school.

"I had orgasms with men, from full body movement with my clothes on. But I made a political decision to not lose control. I kept the touching above my waist, and never dated anyone for more than six weeks. The pleasure was hot and neat—but I still cut them off at six weeks. But then I met Terry. For some reason this young man seemed to be intent on showing me that men were not animals. He brought about the biggest change in me. At the beach, the Eastern shore, we slept together with our clothes off, with a lot of touching and kissing and petting and orgasms at the clitoral level, but we never had intercourse. He softened me, showed me you can share a relationship. I wasn't the hard-assed radical anymore.

"Then I met my husband, the only man I've had intercourse with. He refused to kiss me on our first date. Eventually we planned to have intercourse. We did it right after my period, at a hotel, and I read a book about it first. He was experienced, didn't rush things, and I had a quick orgasm with oral sex.

"Sex has always been good between us, but maybe there was a big physiological change when I was about thirty. I got more horny, and I've gotten more vaginal in my orgasms, and more multiple—I usually have a couple to five now. Even so, I can remember only two times in my life when I've failed to have an orgasm."

For most of the women in this study, becoming orgasmic on an easy, consistent basis involved the firm formation of a personal sexual identity, learning specific skills, and then freely using those skills—all as part of growing and maturing.

Some women feel "born free," and also experience a good balance of closeness and autonomy within their families. When they sexually come of age, these women experience orgasm with a partner within a relatively brief time, and become consistently orgasmic soon after. Women who had a sexually "closed" or anxious mother, but identified very little with her (they often felt closer to fathers or another adult figure) also became orgasmic at a fairly early age, as did women who were forced to be self-reliant by unhappy life situations.

A woman needs assurance that becoming a sexual person will not break the strands of her relationships. A mother's or father's positive communication about sexuality—generally, as well as its specific meaning for their daughter—helps a woman accept her right to personal sexual fulfillment.

## *Soaring Joy: First Orgasm*

Ursula is fifty-nine, a hardy, handsome blonde of German heritage, who was raised on a farm in Kansas:

"I was child number five, smack in the middle of nine. With farm animals and a child every two years, sex was just there. We talked about sex with school friends and relatives, and my mother had a medical dictionary, which was really her downfall; every one of us found it, looking for information on sex. I thought sex was a perfectly normal, pleasurable act."

After graduating from high school, Ursula moved to Topeka by herself: "I've always been self-sufficient and maybe a little obstinate, and I made my own rules about where I would work, and I made my own rules about sex. Probably because of my Catholic upbringing, I believed that intercourse was for marriage, but I petted below the waist, and sometimes touched my partner, but always with our clothes on. These were *my* rules, remember. Around this time I began to read more about sex—library books and romances—and I discovered masturbation. That's when I changed the rules—petting to orgasm was okay, so long as we kept our clothes on."

She remained a virgin until her wedding night. "I enjoyed

intercourse—yet sex, overall, was a little disappointing for both of us. We were shy, had a good case of nerves going, and, without our clothes on, were unsure of what to do and what would really excite us. But then we opened up and were honest, though even then it took me a while to experience regular orgasms. . . .

"My own satisfaction comes first, but we still share our sexual happiness. He's a nice guy and I want him to stay—he's stayed for thirty-four years."

For many women, masturbation helped them become familiar and comfortable with their own reactions and feelings. Ninety percent of the women in this study have masturbated at one time or another, most continue to do so, and some 60 percent feel that there are similarities between their favored stimulation or body position in masturbation and the stimulation or position that best helps them obtain orgasm with a partner. However, if a woman is uncomfortable with masturbation, there certainly is no imperative to do it; a substantial minority, some 25 percent, became easily orgasmic with little or no assistance from their masturbation experience.

Of sixty women, thirty-one had decidedly negative or indifferent feelings about their first intercourse, and fourteen women (like Natalie) felt strongly mixed emotions and/or physical sensations. Only fifteen women reported unmitigated positive feelings. In *all* these cases, whether the relationship was marital, long-term, or casual, the *woman herself* made a complete, personal, and conscious decision that she wanted to have intercourse. She was ready; it was her own choice; she did not give in to pressure, nor require alcohol or drugs to allay her fears. These fifteen women also became consistently orgasmic with a partner within a median of a week or two—much more rapidly than did the group as a whole.

Though a woman's first intercourse is often disappointing,

she almost always finds her first orgasm with a partner to be an experience of pleasure and power:

> I loved him, anticipated the moment for years—but God, I was still surprised to be so multiply orgasmic!

> A great, light, floating feeling that made me more open to pleasure and joy.

> I was shocked with delight.

> Once I had one, I had three. I remember the exact date—and room thirteen at a nearby motel!

> A tremendous, pulsating, forceful thing, an enormous bodily feeling. I wanted to get it again.

Though a handful of women, 10 percent, were frightened by their sensations or felt mixed emotions, they all, naturally, eventually enjoyed the pleasures and feelings of orgasm.

## *Helpful and Key Partners*

A substantial minority of women felt that they themselves had taken the initiative in becoming consistently orgasmic with a partner. Two women explain:

> I learned by myself. I read books and magazines, and took a course on human sexuality. Partners did *not* tell me what to do. I knew what I knew, and cued into my body responses and gathered experience.

> I never had an orgasm until I was married for a few years. It felt terrific, but they weren't regular occurrences, and I decided I'd better do more to bring them on. I just figured that I could do it. It's like

driving a car, you know—when I wanted to drive a car
and I saw all the people driving cars, I thought, "Well,
if they can do it, I can do it."

Others learned, over time, with several considerate lovers,
but the great majority of women learned to be easily orgasmic
with the help of one particular partner.

Meredith, in her mid-thirties, was well advanced in her second pregnancy at the time of our interview. She is strikingly
beautiful, holds a graduate degree in psychology, and her parents are "observant Christians," conservative Presbyterians.
Her low-pitched voice projects confidence and humor:

"Sex was something you didn't discuss, and you never had
sex before marriage, but my parents encouraged me to read
about it. Yet there weren't that many books available, except
the very technical like Kinsey's. I grew up in the fifties and the
sixties and it was still pretty much the Donna Reed ideal—
mothers were at home cooking dinner in white gloves and
pearls.

"I was a late bloomer. Little girls do wiggle in their seat, and
I remember reading books and getting nice feelings, but I never
consciously knew I was masturbating until college. I'll never
forget. In college I went to this talk by some psychologist who
was lecturing about sexuality in women, and she commented
that women masturbate almost as frequently as do men. I was
with my roommate and I remember saying, '*Women* do it too?'
She looked at me and said, 'You'll learn.' Well, I did, really
fast."

Meredith's first intercourse occurred soon after getting engaged to her husband: "I may have consciously made the decision that I was going to have sex with him that night, but at
the same time I didn't have to make it because I was drunk. I'm
sure I thought, 'Well, I was drunk, so I wasn't responsible.'
That absolved me from the guilt. The next night I thought,
'Well, I'm already ruined!' and we made love, but that was *my*

decision, and I had an orgasm. But you see, I never accepted responsibility for myself. Even though I felt I was an independent person, I would defer to my husband or to my boyfriend or to my father.

"After that second night it was very hit and miss, and after we were married it was nothing, a big letdown, less than half the times with an orgasm. Maybe it wasn't as exciting when it was legal. And I used to worry about the vaginal odor, that he'd find it displeasing. You have to be trusting that your partner is going to accept everything, not be turned off by a normal, natural, human bodily thing. And if sometimes it felt good, it was more by luck or chance; I wasn't free enough to let him know.

"After about a year I decided it was for the birds, and we had this big discussion. He was very responsive, like 'Let's work this out,' and we read a whole lot and made a contract together. We agreed that I needed more time, and I demanded an hour just for me, to get myself in the mood. It worked right away and slowed the whole process—I didn't feel I was holding things up —and we discovered what felt good and what didn't. Now, to get in the mood, I only need a few minutes—I know my own feelings and, mentally, I even know how to arouse myself.

"The way we relate sexually is a trump card in our marriage. I feel comfortable, that we're good together. It has taken time, six, seven years, but we could have been back on square one if we hadn't decided it was something to work on together. I think it's a big part of marriage, of any long-standing relationship. I think sex holds it together."

Now and then, a partner was so important to a woman's sexual development that he (or she) became a "key partner," one who helped a woman radically change her sexual attitudes, techniques, and orgasmic capacity.

Wendy had such a partner, a man who also helped heal the wounds of a past savage encounter. She is single and twenty-five, from a Jewish background, darkly exotic, with huge blue eyes that appear dreamy and wistful. She conveys a trusting, vulnerable quality that stems, perhaps, from her "living on the edge" as a serious, creative artist. "I'd like to help other women," she said. "I became nonorgasmic and hated men—there's plenty out there like me.

"I was the oldest of four children. My parents raised all of us to go out and explore. I drew designs for my clothes when I was little, and my mother would make patterns. I thought this was wonderful—she gave me all this power to design what I wanted. We children also picked our own furniture, painted our rooms, took care of our pets—yet our parents weren't quite ready for how we turned out!

"I won art competitions in high school, felt the boys were jerks there, and was a virgin when I left. When I masturbated, I never had any feelings of 'This is wrong or this is right.' It felt comfortable, pleasing, appropriate.

"When I was fifteen, I ran away from home for a few days with a close girlfriend, to New York. We had an 'affair' there, just once, and I was orgasmic with oral sex. I didn't think of it 'sexually'; the closeness was nice, and the tenderness, the sharing. Women make love differently from men and women together, more because they want to be close and please each other, but it's not so much a *sexual* pleasing, at least not for me —I'm usually not orgasmic unless a man's there. I guess I'm bisexual, not 'lesbian,' though I don't really like to label myself. I don't look at women and say, 'Oh, that's a sexually attractive woman.' I might look at her and say, 'Oh, she's beautiful! I'd like to paint her as a pre-Raphaelite angel.' "

At seventeen, Wendy went to Europe as an exchange student. She became involved with a man who lived near her school. "We finally had sex, the biggest anticlimactic thing of my life. It hurt so bad I wanted to stop in the middle, and I remember thinking 'This is what I waited all this time for? This is no big deal!' Then we broke up. He thought if I was his once, I was still his. He got drunk one day and raped me. I fought him off, but he bruised and forced me.

"I didn't have any kind of closeness with a man again until I was about twenty or twenty-one. I wouldn't even let my father hug me. I didn't want to be touched.

"I returned to the States and went to art school in New York. I healed slowly. After a few years I began to like a man, Chris, a student who was my friend. I decided to become sexual again. I also had real hot feelings toward another man, though I never slept with him. I liked his art a lot. Someone who's brilliant or talented is the sexiest thing there is. I had this idea that if you sleep with someone who really knows how to use blue and green, you're going to pick up his energy and become a better painter!

"Chris became my lover for a year. It was hard for me. I had orgasms on occasion, but I still held back because I was so angry. I learned about oral sex and enjoyed giving it, perhaps because I wanted to stay in control. I was always trying this power thing, my attitude wasn't good yet.

"Then I went upstate, to live and paint in the Catskills. There I met Zarek. He was older, unmarried, sort of a Buddhist monk type, the most important man in my sexual life. I told him I wanted to sleep with him, and he wouldn't for the longest time. I'd never had anyone turn me down before—not that I was anything so hot, but I thought this was against the male credo! He wanted to have a real relationship, wanted to know me— all those things I had thought were bullshit.

"He was very erotic in everything he did. In the beginning I wasn't consistent with my orgasms. I found myself subconsciously blocking, as if I couldn't help it anymore. I'd let myself come to a peak, try to let go . . . and couldn't. He understood all my blocks. He'd sit there and tell me we had to do T'ai Chi [Chinese rhythmic movements that release bodily energy], or we had to travel to Oregon and see a therapist there, or he'd do Shiatsu [a Japanese massage therapy] to relieve my sexual tension. He was also a good lover as far as stamina; he could wait for me—or he knew if it would be to no avail! He read *The Story of O* to me and said, 'This is not only about sadomasochism, this is about a woman who loves her man so much that he says follow me, and she says okay, I'll follow you without asking questions.' I was naive about relationships and emotions and he taught me. He taught me about sex as if I was a virgin—and with him I really was because I trusted him completely. Maybe I had done things previously, but I had never *felt* them. He was the first man I let myself go with. I trusted him enough to explore with him. I really *participated* in sex.

"Yes, he was very special. Somehow I didn't fall in love, which surprised me. I moved away from the Catskills, but we still write each other, and I think of him more as a teacher now than simply a bygone lover."

Sometimes a long-term relationship can undergo a radical transformation, from being almost "asexual," to being lushly erotic.

Julia's sexual awakening forged a new marital balance. She is thirty-four, married for fifteen years, a full-figured woman of average height, who strengthens and tones her body through jogging and isometrics. Her features are pretty and delicate, her manner, at first, reserved. "Don't get me wrong," she began, "we still have some problems. But I wanted to tell someone. Sex has helped my marriage.

"I was the oldest of four children. My parents were Methodist and Lutheran, and made a big deal out of never discussing sex with me. My husband was the first guy I necked with. Then we made love in a car—I remember holding back because I feared getting caught or pregnant. We married when I was nineteen. We were churchgoing—my brother's a Methodist minister—had grown up in the community, and were active in community service. We seemed a close family, and both of us worked in the business my husband and I had established, one still fairly prosperous.

"Until two years ago, I might have had an orgasm one time in ten. I enjoyed sex to a point, but I still felt it was dirty. I had sex to have children, at least until my little girl was born, and it seemed every time I would sneeze, I'd get pregnant. I was tense, a missionary-position girl—that was *it*—and there was still something blocking me, until I unwound and realized that sex was an enjoyable experience.

"We were having some problems, and my husband had started to see another girl. I knew that he was doing this, and I didn't want to lose him. He would come home at three or four in the morning and . . . somehow it excited me. I was angry of course, but I had this real funny feeling that I just had to have him, that I needed him to be with me. I became very aroused waiting up for him, excited that he'd been with another woman. We began to make love more, from once or twice a week to at least once a night. I needed the attention, and gave more of myself. I had never gone for oral sex, and started getting into that, enjoyed it, and it just seemed that everything started to flow. He'd get worked up, and it would get my insides working too, and it seemed every step brought another.

"I have six to a dozen orgasms now. He talks to me, acting out some role like a rape scene. Like he'll pretend he's a repairman, make advances, take advantage of me, ask me, 'How would your husband like your doing this?' Or else I'm his street-girl whore—I wear black nylons and garter belts, he's my pimp in my mind, and he forces me to take other men in his presence. Or other times he's sweet, I'm an innocent little thing, and then we hardly talk, we just make love. Then it's the feel, the touch.

"I used to have to be tied up—it got me hot and helped me break through—and we still do bondage maybe half the time, though I'm getting to like it better now without that. It's like drinking. I had to drink before, to be able to get aroused, whereas now I don't drink anything—not even soda pop. We have leather straps and chains, and a leather swing my husband made, one he's able to hang from our bedroom ceiling; and he chains me to the wall, our bed, or the huge steel frame of an exercise gym we keep in our recreation room. Sometimes I'm so excited, I rip out the chains when I come. I'm not into pain —a little's okay—but as soon as he starts tying me up, I can feel my body becoming tingly. Just the idea of it, maybe because I can't do anything; I know that no matter how much he stimulates me, if I say, 'Stop, I can't take it anymore,' I couldn't stop him if I wanted to. Just the thought of it . . .

"And I've had orgasms getting him aroused, without ever really touching myself. Just talking to him, asking if it's getting him excited, with oral sex, or if he's chained and I'm whipping him and he's moving around, and moaning and saying, 'Oh, it's good, it's good . . .'—just everything. I get excited knowing he's satisfied."

Then Julia and her husband began to go out together, picking up men in bars. "The first was a spur-of-the-moment thing, a guy liking my cleavage. I was worried I'd get hurt, but it worked well, the man was gentle and caring, and we did it many times, two men making love to me. If we knew him well, we'd let him take me in bondage. Then we began to swing, in clubs or with groups of people, and then I first made love with another woman. She excited me, our lives seemed parallel, and we made each other come with oral love. Sex with others is secondary—it isn't love, but fun, and excites us at home. Sometimes he's jealous, but I always need him to start me off, and always want him near me.

"I had over one hundred orgasms one evening. He counted. Sometimes my comes were a game to him, and he loves to see me worked up. It was one of those nights when I was really high without drinking. My muscles, I guess, were so relaxed, such that he'd touch me and I'd just go off, then someone else, and someone else, and I'd come. . . . Anything would set me off, even a brush against me, I was gone, completely off. It was the people we were with, at a club. Everyone was talking, having a good time. We've had friends at home, but our excitement's been higher since we went to the club. We'd drive home and be so excited that we had to do it again, and sometimes we couldn't get all the way home, but pulled to the side of the road. . . ."

In order to help her marriage and develop her sexuality, Julia has made choices that would hardly suit most women—but her choices, thus far, have been right *for her*. She *enjoys* her sexuality, and her acts occur with a man she trusts, express her own desires, and are actually within her control. And, she is responsible toward their children: "We are careful to protect them from our sex life."

One additional comment. Because of a newly reawakened fear of sexually transmitted diseases—such as chlamydia, herpes, and AIDS—several women who had participated in group, multipartner, or casual, less-selective, single-partner sex indicated that they have recently restricted these activities.

How can a partner help a woman to be orgasmic? We asked the women whether there was one "quality" or "technique" in making love that an ideal partner should have. Impressively, even within the context of obtaining a specific and limited sexual objective, her orgasm, most every woman alluded to relationship qualities; specific techniques were secondary. (We discovered a noteworthy exception, involving the moments preceding orgasm, for every woman in this study. See Chapter 10.) Every woman has preferences, and an artful lover is precious, but apparently, if a partner has the qualities below, he will easily learn—provided she expresses them—a woman's needs and desires.

Four general qualities, often overlapping, emerged from their responses:

- Showing tenderness, caring, affection, consideration, and sensitivity toward her: "Affection—men in touch with their female aspects make superb lovers."

"Gentleness and tenderness, conveying affection in a natural way."

- Communication: "A partner who takes time to learn what I like, and who talks with me—don't just leave me on my own, please." "It's important to have a friendship before being lovers. I need open communication to arouse me, so I won't be embarrassed when I really let go."

- Accepting her desires and preferences, being nonjudgmental, making her feel comfortable: "My best partners relax me, accept me, and show they enjoy our lovemaking." "I need him to not make me feel I'm kinky, to accept me—my creative and intellectual sides, my passion."

- Promoting trust in *him,* making *her* feel secure: "Make me feel comfortable and important—I need to feel trust in my partner." "I become more orgasmic when I trust a man."

And, as one woman wryly states, an ounce of spontaneity is also highly valued:

At first he was the type of guy that, once he went off, he went in the bathroom, took a complete shower, came in with his jammies on, and went to bed. That was it. No hugging, kissing, nothing. Then he became so mechanical! He started reading magazines, and a book on *male* sexuality. Then it was ten minutes of foreplay, ten minutes of intercourse, ten minutes of kissing her good night, ten minutes of going into the shower and going back to bed—I could feel exactly what he was going by, he went by the goddamn book!

# Becoming Consistent: 2
# Three Principles

Together you ride right through it.

*—Ingrid*

Female orgasm is neither a fragile nor difficult experience. After all, orgasmic response is a natural physiological function. But all too often that natural response is blocked by inhibition, or by simple lack of knowledge.

We asked the women how they first freed their natural response to become easily orgasmic. For women orgasmic right from the start, we asked for their reflections on how they felt it had been accomplished.

For *all* women, the answers emerged with consistency and centered around three principles. They are worth keeping in mind as you read the following chapters, as each may come into play at various stages of lovemaking.

## *Principle Number One: Accept Your Total Self— Body, Mind, and Genitals*

Psychological barriers, inhibiting guilts or fears, caused many women to "hold back" from joyfully sharing sex.

Harriet is a social worker, a large, gentle woman from a Methodist and Nazarene background: "We argued over sex the first few years we were married. My husband talked sex in the middle of sex—which made me feel *guilty* and totally wrecked

my feelings. And he wanted to experiment, try new positions
—I wasn't gung ho for any of it. I thought that sex was hor-
mones, you had them or you didn't. . . .

"It helped when we moved to Texas, away from my relatives.
I didn't fear someone walking in, and I talked with other
women—though certain exciting things, like anal stimulation,
still caused guilty feelings. But then, as I got free of taboos, we
could discuss our sexuality. I learned I could set up a mood and
ask for what felt good to me, and the more I applied my mind,
the more I'd get out of sex."

Erica, single and in her early twenties, is a sculptor who is
currently completing a graduate degree in art history: "I really
had some hang-ups. I was nineteen and at college, and sex was
something wonderful, terrific—but evil. Black seemed appropriate for sex, and I had a bunch of black dresses and shawls
and things that I wore on sexy dates. I didn't know about love
and love playing, intimacy, and those aspects of a relationship.
I didn't know about the really nice things, like morning-after
rolls and coffee in bed. Sex was always associated with night,
and a passionate, reckless encounter."

"Good girl" guilts were a hindrance for other women:

All my life I heard "This or that's not good, don't do
it." At first I was very hesitant—"good girl" thoughts
came into my head whenever I got excited.

I held back—nice little girls didn't come from oral sex,
and certainly not with their husbands. When I was
engaged, I had an affair with a black man, and came
all over when he ate me out—killed two taboos with
that one. After eight years of marriage, and routine
sex, I had another affair. I would leave my lover before
dinner, fresh out of bed, feeling so good, so high and
excited, and when my husband came home, I would
try to involve him in my feelings. We'd have sex, but it

wasn't the same level. I couldn't approach him. I couldn't let that wild person out.

Sometimes early guilts can be turned to sexual advantage. Dorothy, a peppery redhead from a Catholic family background, was nonorgasmic with her husband through her first several years of marriage: "I was always Miss Goody Two-Shoes as a kid. So—wow!—when I discovered when I was lying on top of him that when he put his hands under the back of my pantyhose and started pulling them down—I don't know what happens to my head, but that almost gives me an orgasm right there. Maybe that goes back to when I was a kid, and first played around with sex. It would have made me feel guilty, and stopped me back then, but now I let it arouse me. I've turned that around into a positive thing. If someone takes my pants down, it really turns me on!

"Another fantasy that I have a lot is watching a movie, maybe a drive-in movie, and getting played with at the same time. It relates back to when I was dating, the first time somebody tried to play with me and I held back—though I'm sure I really wanted to let him do it. But now, rather than the 'no-no's,' I'm fantasizing being in that same position—and letting the good part happen!"

Fears can be equally restraining. Meredith, the beautiful woman described in Chapter 1, who demanded an hour just for herself, remembers both guilt and fear: "I was afraid of my passion. I feared that underneath I was a seething nymphomaniac."

Many women experience a fear of their normal bodily sensations. Constance, a factory worker, is a pert, outgoing redhead who is in her early thirties: "I never masturbated, and I didn't understand the sensations. It was two years after my first intercourse that I reached the first orgasm I ever had in my life—I actually saw colors, collapsed on him, and cried because I was scared. After that I was always orgasmic; I became more aggressive, if you will, and made sure I got on top. I thought to myself, 'I am going to experience this more often, there is nothing wrong with it, it's wonderful. Anything this good, there's got to be a way of repeating.' I never feared them once I understood what they were."

Two other women relate:

I needed about six months of intercourse with my husband before I knew what to expect and felt comfortable with my body. That I wasn't going to do something disgusting, like pee all over the place with that strong orgasmic response I have. Or worry about feeling embarrassed if I started screaming like a maniac. I would lose total control of my body, and didn't know what would happen.

I learned that his stimulating my clitoris really added a lot. I mean, he always did it before, but I pushed him away because it gave me a weird feeling. When he would touch me there, I would get nervous or something, and tell him, "No!" I would shy away from things I didn't know about.

Accepting herself is accepting her body, with its flaws and imperfections. Darcie, thirty-one, is divorced ("He always thought he was *right,* period—he even *redid my laundry!*"). After her divorce, she had a quick orgasm with the first man she dated: "Right at that point I said to myself, 'If this can be so wonderful, so beautiful, and I just met this fellow, *what have I been doing all these years?*' And I said to myself, 'There's someone else in there who wants to get out, and I'm going to let her out!' "

She describes her loving ritual: "When I'm nude, and completely isolated in the bedroom, I will look at myself up and down in the mirror. Now, I wish I had a bigger bust, and maybe I'm on the slender side—maybe some men don't like that. But I say to myself, 'Darcie, don't just look at your body, look at yourself as a person, look at your personality. And I find the best parts of my body, the sexy hollows and curves.

"Now, another woman might tell me, 'Well, sure, Darcie, you can talk about that—look at you, you skinny thing.' I hear that all the time. But a woman has to accept herself. She shouldn't see herself as fat, or with bulges, but just as a little bit voluptuous. They have more on top than I do—that's for sure!—and I show how they have a nice bust line, and with it a bit more flesh here and there, but all together it's nice. She has to look at the good parts, she has to look at *herself.*"

Accepting herself is accepting her body, everywhere. Many women have particular difficulty embracing their natural genital beauty. Through trust in her husband's pleasure, Meredith learned to accept her vagina, and all her sexual fluids, as a "normal, natural, human bodily thing," a source not of odor but of fragrance. Other women had similar experiences. According to one: "I finally liked my pussy. You have to be able to touch yourself, be comfortable with your body, with excitement and sensual feelings."

Yet even among these easily orgasmic women, total self-acceptance falls far short of "perfect." Take the case of Emily, a sales manager in her late twenties: "I can't have an orgasm with masturbation. It's probably old guilt, just like oral sex. I know I'm hung up about that; I can't get myself to relax enough. My mother, you know, would always say, 'Get your hands away from there, don't do that.' She never said oral sex, of course, it was just her attitude. She used to talk to my brother and father about stuff like that. 'You just don't do that; nice women don't do that. You don't ever go down on a man, that's disgusting.' She made me feel it was dirty. That's probably why, if my husband's going to go down on me—I know this is weird —but I have to take a shower first."

And another woman states: "I still have problems, sometimes, letting myself let go. I seem to censor myself as to what is 'proper' and not wanton." During our interviews, several women needed assurance that their perfectly normal behaviors were not "weird" or abnormal. Other women have sexual desires with which they are still uncomfortable, or which they are afraid to act upon. Several barely accept their genitals—and more find fault with their bodies. Unfortunately, a woman's weight and body shape is often the *critical* element of her feelings of self-esteem.

In terms of self-acceptance, many of these women still face "unfinished business," yet nearly all suggest that strides toward self-acceptance—of body, mind, and genitals—are a necessary prelude to becoming easily orgasmic.

## *Principle Number Two: Let It Be—Allow Your Pleasure to Happen*

According to the women in this study, it's up to *them* to obtain their own orgasm—if not entirely, then equally with their partners. As one says:

> He can stimulate me all he wants, and if I'm not in the mood, nothing is going to happen. Since the woman's orgasm is different, it's her responsibility to let go, to let her body be receptive to having an orgasm.

And another woman:

> Through getting my clitoris in position, I can almost do it myself. But I've got to be there mentally, not just physically.

We asked the women the following question: Do you ever make a conscious decision to "go for orgasm," and then feel it's right to use your partner's body at that time to obtain it?

Despite the strong wording (*use* your partner's body), fifty-six of sixty women said yes. A few typical comments:

I establish my own body rhythm before orgasm and think of satisfying myself only.

Sure, just like he's using mine. It's part of his commitment as a sex partner.

We both do—that's what it's all about, pleasing each other.

When I acknowledge to my brain that I'm going for orgasm, it's my takeover and very easy.

Just before, when you know there's no turning back, going for it is of prime importance.

Some of the yes's were qualified, usually revolving around the issue of how conscious the decision was—"I usually don't think when I'm that aroused"—or, most often, the terminology: "When I have sex, I've already made the decision to have an orgasm, but 'using your partner's body' sounds selfish." "It's self-evident—but I'm not exploiting my lover." The few "no" answers involved similar issues, as well as that of "naturalness": "Orgasm is just part of what I am doing."

Although easily orgasmic women "go for" orgasm, they are also keenly aware that orgasm is not a goal in itself, that striving for it is usually self-defeating, and that anxious worries about "performance" spell the end of pleasure. Instead, the women have learned to make orgasm *possible.*

Dorothy, the peppery redhead, expresses a number of these points: "I couldn't find the right combination. My idea of being good in bed was making *him* feel good—forgetting all about *me.* Or if I was trying to achieve an orgasm, that was all I thought of. Then I finally realized that turning myself on turns him on, and it's okay to enjoy it, and it's okay to position yourself right, and it's okay to tell somebody what feels good and what doesn't. I realized I was ninety percent of it."

Ursula, the woman brought up on a farm in Kansas: "Don't think about your orgasm or you will foul it up."

Meredith again: "That's half the secret of having an orgasm. If you know it's going to come, if you don't worry about whether you're going to have one or not, you will."

And other women:

You don't *have to* have an orgasm—just enjoy yourself and allow it to happen.

Relax, relax, don't try too hard.

You can't say you're going to "get" an orgasm; you need to relax and let go.

Orgasm just happens, you can't strive for it. And it's just no problem if it doesn't happen.

There are, as always, nuances of personal preference: "It depends on my mood and the situation. Sometimes I really go for it, and sometimes I let it take me."

## Principle Number Three: Let Go—Surrender Yourself to Nature

"Letting it take me" may well be the key.

Ingrid is thirty-one and married, a slightly plump blonde with mischievous eyes. She was well-prepared for our interview: "I've been practicing all week! But then, I can remember only four occasions in my life when I haven't had an orgasm.

"My parents were strict, but all us kids were loners, and we sort of raised ourselves, pretty much outside the home. And somewhere I got the attitude that you have to please yourself first; if it feels good, it must be okay. Before we married, I had lots of orgasms with my husband from petting. Amazing! At first I thought you had to be *married* to have orgasms! I was a virgin on our wedding night, but I came all over the place from intercourse, very nice and natural. . . .

"In the middle of intercourse, I don't have worries or fears or doubts, I don't fight anything about it, and just before my climax I concentrate on sensations. It's a free feeling, an abandonment. . . . Enjoy, relax, and go with it. . . ."

Letting go, abandoning the self to sensation, was the one essential that every woman mentioned. However practiced her technique or focused her effort, at the golden moment she rarely strives for orgasm. Instead, if she "works" for anything, she works to build her sensation—bigger, stronger, and deeper, enveloping all of her being—and *gives herself up to nature.*

Before they became easily orgasmic, many women's fears centered on "control" and trust, or "losing" a part of the self:

I tend to be a person who likes to be in control. It's scary to let go and trust a partner—I'm never more open and vulnerable than when I'm giving myself.

I feared allowing a partner to "take an orgasm out of my body"—that somehow I wouldn't be there when making love was over. It was like there was a black pit on the other side. Go too far, and you may not know how to get back.

Letting go is giving trust, and relinquishing control:

I was always very orgasmic, but then I had a bad relationship. I became afraid that if I showed my true self, something bad would happen. I had to learn to trust my husband, to let go, to let myself feel sensations.

Trust is a big factor. In other areas of my life, I'm a very controlled person. But in making love, in a way I work to lose control and just allow it to happen. At orgasm, it's pleasantly giving up control.

Trust and relax or you freeze it. To come, I give up control, and let my partner take it.

Letting go is an "active" mode with the flavor of concentration:

I focus into sensation, sometimes even my partner's, and stay in the here and now.

I concentrate on my partner's body touching me, how good it feels, how good his penetration, how good the sensations and image.

Think of the sexual parts of your body, how your breasts are tautly quivering, how your vagina is filled.

I concentrate on building to a peak, the rising heat of my body, the feeling of being swelled.

Letting go is also a "receptive" mode, allowing yourself to "flow," to merge with sensation:

I'm floating, only aware of my feelings.

Relax, go with what feels good, allow your body sensations to flow, give yourself the freedom of total expression in movement.

It's total relaxation, giving up inhibitions, letting loose and letting go, flowing into sensations.

Then the sensations take over, go on, and then I just
go with them.

And, for many easily orgasmic women, letting go is surrender:

It's total abandonment, a feeling of being caught up in
giving.

I concentrate solely wherever I'm touched—you have
to surrender your senses.

At orgasm, I just push out and sort of let go.
Whatever the stimulation is that brought you there,
you continue. Surrender yourself to that feeling.

Maybe until orgasm you're sort of holding back, but
then you have to just give in to the feeling. That's the
time of surrendering.

You are surrendering your body to your partner at
orgasm. It's the same way if a woman brings a man to
orgasm, she has that power over him, and I'm sure the
male feels the same way. It's a surrendering.

I try to establish a mood, a willingness to submit my
body to anything.

And, of course, letting go is often a blend of all these varied
approaches, concentration and giving up control, flowing and
surrender.

3

# Personal Patterns

I had to accept doing it *my* way.

—*Nora*

Nora, a single woman in her early thirties, has a slight but sturdy body and a raconteur's gift for gab. She teaches mentally handicapped adults, having attained a specialized graduate degree for that purpose. Her father died when Nora was in early adolescence, leaving a family of five children, of which Nora is the third oldest. Her motivation to participate in the research project stemmed from a friend's recent revelation that, even within a loving relationship, she had never been orgasmic in seventeen years of marriage.

Nora's early ideas about sexuality (you pray to heaven for babies) came from nuns at a Catholic school; at the onset of menstruation her mother took a hand in her education. Nora recalls: "Right then and there she said, 'I better tell you about sex. You know a boy has a penis,' and she explained it, putting it very simply. 'And the man puts his penis inside the woman, they make love . . . ,' all very basic, and I looked at her and said, 'I don't believe you.' She said, 'Well, it's true.' And I said, 'I can't believe people do that!' I guess it was because I was so old by the time I learned anything, that it was a shock. But her attitude was real positive and conveyed it was all very normal."

However "normal," intercourse was proper only in marriage; so Nora concentrated on friendship and intellectual development, kissing a boy for the first time on her sixteenth birthday.

Describing herself as "very organized" about sex, in her early twenties she decided that if by age twenty-five she was not yet married, she would have intercourse anyway. She masturbated for the first time at age twenty-three: "It was the neatest feeling, and then the fascination that this information was in my body and I'd never utilized it—wow!"

As she approached her twenty-fourth birthday, Nora began to suspect that virginity was an overrated pleasure: "I decided to have sex, and conned a girlfriend into giving me a month's prescription of birth-control pills in time to be covered on New Year's Eve. I had a date for New Year's with someone I liked very much, a nice guy and good friend. I knew he would try, and, poor man, unbeknownst to him, I just let him go ahead. The minute he entered me, I burst into tears and he goes, 'What's the matter? What's the matter?' and I said, 'I'm not a virgin anymore,' and he goes, 'Oh no! Oh no! Nora, how could you let me do this to you?' and I said, 'No, I wanted you to.' Anyway, that was how I had sex the first time. I would advise anyone to wait as I did, because it was my decision, I was ready. I didn't feel pressure and I didn't feel guilt.

"My body goes extremely rigid when I orgasm. Yet men implied I could orgasm certain ways—with my legs in the air. It wasn't not only not my style, *it was not practical,* but I tried for a year or two and maybe I almost came that way once or twice until I decided they were wrong. I was so worried about how I was 'supposed' to do it, it was taking away the pleasure. I think that's very important for women because I've met a couple who have said something comparable, and my advice is always the same: You have to get your partner to understand that that's how you're going to enjoy it, and he's got to let you do it *your way.*

"For my own orgasm, if I want to come during intercourse, I have to control it by getting myself in a particular position, basically on my back, and sort of shuffle my partner around to where it's comfortable and feels good. I can't imagine letting some man come in and have sex with me in whatever sort of way he wanted, and not really doing anything—I probably wouldn't come. And once I start into orgasm, I have to just let myself go. Sometimes I'm into it deeply enough to quickly have two or three more."

You might say that Nora is organized but flexible—she had her first orgasm with a partner on her twenty-fifth birthday, exactly.

Her story illuminates an oft-told tale of the partner who thinks he knows a woman's needs better than she does herself. As another woman described it:

> I think most guys have preconceived notions of what women like, and they're going to do that for you whether you like it or not. It bugs me that they haven't taken the time to find out that women are different and they like different things. Maybe this turns somebody else on, but it doesn't do a thing for me—it's a turnoff. When it happens, I think, "Well, some woman must have enjoyed that—but it wasn't me, baby!"

## Sexual Style

It is essential for a woman to experience, recognize, and accept her own sexual style. Every woman has personal patterns of emotional, mental, and physical stimulation that she aesthetically prefers, and that she finds most effective in bringing her to orgasm.

Sexuality is an ongoing, changing experience. At the time of our interview, few women were the "same" sexually as they had been three or five years previously, and many expressed hopes and goals for the future—to be "more open," to experiment more, to explore their desires and fantasies, to better integrate sex within a stable relationship.

A woman's sexual style also changes. Change may occur

over time, in cycles of months or years. As one woman explains:

> You change. . . . I've changed before pregnancy, after
> pregnancy, when I'm fat, when I'm thin. My feelings
> about my body and erogenous zones change.

Or a woman with different partners:

> With some men, I get in the mood by acting a role.
> With others, if I'm falling short in the buildup to
> orgasm, I'll fantasize more.

With the same partner from encounter to encounter:

> Sometimes I want a lot of pressure and other times I
> want him to be gentle with me.

Over the course of one encounter:

> You have to express your changing moods and let
> them control your sexual needs.

In addition to recognizing and accepting her current—and possibly only momentary—sexual style, an easily orgasmic woman usually finds a means of communicating her changing preferences to partners. However, she does not necessarily reveal *all* aspects of her sexual style, particularly those that are entirely within her mental province. Effective communication is often a matter of need, discretion, and taste.

Sometimes a woman's understanding of herself runs counter to her perceptions of prevailing wisdom; in this event, most easily orgasmic women have learned to *trust themselves,* though not without some difficulty and temporary confusion. For example, two women on the same subject:

One of the things that threw me off when I was trying to find a way to regularly achieve orgasm, was reading that all stimulation is in the clitoris and that you only imagine stimulation inside the vagina. After quite a bit of experience, I decided that they're crazy!

I don't know why I felt my orgasms were vaginal, because in most of the books that I've read, it's usually clitoral stimulation, and I thought, "Well, somebody put me together wrong."

Lisa, a chic, dynamic young woman in her mid-twenties, is aptly described as black, bright, and beautiful. She is a documentary film editor who harbors an ambition to become an on-camera TV news reporter; chances are you'll see her someday, while you are watching TV in your living room.

Lisa grew up as the middle child of five brothers and sisters. She was raised to be independent, a high achiever, a leader in her family and at school. Older siblings and friends often sought her counsel. Her mother's attitude about sex was "positive but private," and sexual information came mainly from her father: "He would never say, 'Okay, everybody, gather 'round, we're going to talk about sex.' We would be watching TV or something and he would gradually get into it, talk about sexuality, about how teenagers like to have sex too, whether their parents want to face up to it or not. There were older children, and I remember him starting this when I was about five. I thought it was pretty great, pretty healthy, and sometimes he may have been a little too zealous, but he always said you had to be responsible. Later, when I was twelve or thirteen, one of the beautiful things about him was he just answered my questions. It wasn't like, 'Oh, why? Are you going to start experimenting?' "

Lisa first had intercourse at the age of fifteen, and, with the same boyfriend, her first orgasm four months later. Following a pattern seen with several other women we interviewed, her boyfriend had been out of town before the encounter and Lisa was mentally and physically primed: "I was really kind of lost in the lovemaking, for once not listening for somebody to interrupt us, when all of a sudden I started feeling strange. I never talked much during sex except to say 'I love you,' but I started to almost rant and rave, something to the effect that if he ever left me, I'd kill him. I felt this tremendous energy inside, and then I started crying."

But the experience produced emotional conflict: "Because I had opened myself up, felt so naked, I really didn't like it in a sense. I consider myself a very cool and level-headed person, and I had acted totally irrationally. I didn't like the crying and the screaming, and he maybe thought, 'Oh wow, she's really crazy about me, and I have some way of reaching this person.' That's the way I saw it, not just sexual enjoyment."

When this relationship terminated, again following a pattern seen in several other women, Lisa was certain her orgasmic days were over, attributing past success to her partner's expertise and an "irreplaceable sexual combination." Within two years she met her present husband and became, in fact, substantially more orgasmic.

Whether minutes, hours, or days in advance of a sexual encounter, Lisa prepares herself mentally: "I learned over time that it's so important for me, thinking about making love. No matter how experienced my partner, if I'm not ready, nothing is going to happen. And now, partly because I've had the same partner for what I consider a long time, nearly seven years dating and married, I have to build up to it and concentrate—and we both have to work at getting each other aroused."

We will describe these events in detail in later chapters, but for now suffice it to say that while making love, Lisa usually sees brief mental images of herself and her husband together, intermixed with close-up images of her body. She also generates a variety of fantasies, "including behaviors I wouldn't do," and a number of roles, some outwardly acted and others purely imagined.

As for her personal sexual style: "Basically, no matter what my behavior or role is, how bizarre or conservative or whatever, I always tell myself deep down inside, 'It's good, it's natural, it's right,' or 'It feels good, it's got to be right.' It *is* right and I don't care what anybody thinks! *Whatever I like is perfectly right.*"

## Assisting Your Own Arousal

Is a woman healthy and sexually "normal" if her mind is erotically active while making love with a partner? Evidence has emerged in the past ten years that answers emphatically, yes.

Until recent years, therapists treating women for psychological problems conceived and formed the bulk of our ideas, both popular and professional, concerning erotic mental activity. Freud stated, "We can begin by saying that happy people never make phantasies, only unsatisfied ones," and psychoanalysts felt, for example, that fantasy, perhaps prompted by fear of the penis, was used by a woman in sex to distance herself from partners. Small wonder the view was negative, particularly when the activity arose while the woman—usually suffering relational problems—was making love with a partner. We now realize that a *majority* of women have fantasies or other mental images *during sexual relations.*

Also in recent years, a number of sex therapy programs, designed to help a woman become more orgasmic, have discarded the notion that mental activity is harmful. Women are encouraged to freely use fantasy, or any reasonable source of erotic mental excitement, to heighten their sexual pleasure.

And then there are the women in our study—easily orgasmic women. Before and throughout the sexual encounter, *they ex-*

*hibit a startling range and depth of erotic mental activity.* Based on the results of our study, a woman whose mind is erotically active while making love with a partner is not only healthy and normal—she is likely to be *orgasmic.*

There is, of course, a purpose to erotic mental activity, a natural, adaptive purpose: It assists a woman's own sexual arousal, and thus facilitates orgasm.

"Assisting her own arousal" does not mean that a woman prefers to be "into herself." To the contrary, an easily orgasmic woman is fully engaged when making love and highly aware of her partner, his pleasures and responses. Nevertheless, she must have the *freedom,* both physical and psychological, to initiate and enhance her own sexual arousal.

During lovemaking, she accepts her erotic thoughts as stemming from her deepest sexuality, and enjoys them at will or generates more—so long as they elevate pleasure. Whatever she tries and doesn't like she blithely discards in an instant.

Recent years have witnessed impressive advances in the technology employed to study sexual arousal and orgasmic response; for example, vaginal sensors measure physiological changes such as vaginal and labial congestion, or vaginal pulsing and contraction. A raft of studies show that women respond with sexual arousal—physiological changes—to audio tapes of erotic stories, erotic films, and self-generated erotic fantasy. When they employ biofeedback, and are instructed "to become as aroused as you can, using erotic thoughts if you like," some women sexually respond whenever they *will* to do so.

Here are some typical comments from women in our study:

*Of course* I arouse myself!

I turn myself on with images.

The mental stuff is *most* important.

I control orgasms with my mind—and have more control with age.

I arouse myself, but the *intensity* of my orgasm
depends on my emotional involvement.

The last comment raises a vital issue. Why not always just
think about your partner, focusing on how much you love him,
and how good and blessed are your bonds of devotion? In our
moral teachings, and in our Western literature of romantic love,
such thoughts are the proper prescription.

Among easily orgasmic women, thoughts of love and care for
a partner are very common arousers, but only one of *many*
events that add to sexual excitement. Further, in the world of
reality, these thoughts are not always true or convincing, and
even in the strongest relationship, emotional care ebbs and
flows. Human beings have a need for variety, novelty, adventure, risk; over the years of a long-term relationship, partners
can find that their love is strong, and yet they've become, if only
for the moment, creatures of habit and sexually bored. Rather
than being "immoral" or "unromantic," a woman's free use of
her body and mind to increase sexual pleasure contributes to
the highest values—living a loving, vigorous life and sharing
that life with another.

## A Portrait of the Woman as an Artist

Easily orgasmic women resemble creative artists. If only for
the briefest of moments, while making love with a partner, they
weave a spell of body and mind to create a joyous experience.

Kristin, in her early thirties, is a psychotherapist who coun-
sels physically ill patients in a private hospital. Her face has a
pleasing Eurasian cast—gray almond eyes half close when she
smiles—but her body is large-boned, physically fit, and she's
aware of her vulnerabilities: "I've always had a problem with
my body, in terms of loving myself. I have a vision of what to
me is beautiful and I don't fit that vision—bigger breasts, longer
legs, slimmer, smaller, more delicate."

She has lived abroad for many years, acquiring a soft English accent. In England she completed the equivalent of a doctorate in psychology, then worked several years as a group therapist and student placement counselor before marrying her husband (from whom she is currently separated). She has two children.

"I was raised as a Presbyterian, rather strictly, and I received a clear message that one does not screw until married. I was close to Mother, though we did not closely communicate, and I had fights with my father, who was usually a mild man. I was both dependent and independent, occasionally a trifle rebellious —perhaps I was shedding them before I realized. I went abroad to study at age eighteen, scared but quickly adjusting.

"My first affair with a man was in Italy. I met him on a train I was taking from Ischia to London. He was beautiful, a medical student. When the train stopped at Florence, he offered me his apartment, a distance away, in Bologna. It was romantic, wonderful, exactly how I had pictured it. He was good, considerate, manipulated well, and I came to feel him as a person. That night—or day—I came the first time, within a span of eight hours from the time we began to make love. We saw each other for two or three years, weeks at a time, in England or Italy. He was my most significant sexual partner, experienced, a doctor. I knew he wouldn't hurt me, and I trusted him completely. I had the quick full course—oral sex, anal intercourse, and physical relations with women.

"I'm also a great and avid reader, and when I started becoming sexually active, I went out and read every book I could find because I wanted to be good in bed. I wanted to know what to do and not do, because my mother certainly didn't tell me about oral sex or anal. As I learned, and then was able to do these with partners, feel more proficient and comfortable, then certainly my ability to be orgasmic became greater. And my ability to enjoy became greater when I felt that not only could I receive, but I could give. Maybe a lot of effort was put into being orgasmic, although I'd not thought about it and had never planned it that way. But now it's easier simply because one is more relaxed.

"If I care for a person, if I feel something, I can become quite orgasmic with someone who is not very sexually adept. I can also be quite orgasmic with someone who's very good, but for whom I have little intimate feeling. But then I have to use a lot more of my own creativity to bring pleasure about. But in any relations with a partner, if I want to be orgasmic, it's up to me to create a blend of mental and physical pleasure."

Mimi, approaching thirty, is an opera performer and teacher who holds a master's in music. She exudes energy, warmth, and strength, and always an aura of glamour.

"I was the oldest of three sisters, and a very identified Jew. I adored and admired my father—always wanted a boy like Daddy—and my mother was like the earth. He was brilliant, an absent-minded professor—which in fact he is, a prominent expert on Russian history. Mother is a businesswoman who agents painters and owns a gallery, doing extremely well. Both were very creative, emotionally open, relaxed, affectionate, and they took the lead in talking about sex. Mother said, 'Just be sure you care,' and Father once said, 'People have sex—if you're turned on, go to bed.' They always supported our independence and let us lead our own lives. I learned to make decisions, then *do* what I decided.

"But I was scared of puberty, like my breasts, embarrassed by my period, and was probably scared of *being a woman* until college. I think I had a little Oedipal father-daughter guilt thing, and my mother told me a story recently—it was never in my mind except maybe subconsciously—that I once walked in while my parents were making love. Mom is pretty vocal in sex, and she told me I thought my father was hurting her. Though I played with myself when young, I never consciously masturbated, and I never dated or petted in high school. I was busy with my music, maybe blocked opportunities, and all my friends were incestuously 'safe'—male, intellectual, and Jewish.

"The first man I met at college became my lover. It was devastating. My body reactions were terribly strong, and the more my body reacted, the more it freaked him out. He thought French kissing was gross, and wouldn't let me touch his genitals. I never felt guilt about intercourse, but he was so uptight that he made me feel lewd, embarrassed, ashamed—that something about me was horrible. I stayed with him almost two years, never had an orgasm, but I did learn one big fear: let myself get too aroused, and a man will back off, frightened. I finally broke away from him, for a man who was very attractive —until I found out both men one and two were sleeping with my roommate. She was the type that kept a black book.

"That was it for men. I was to spend that summer performing at a music festival on the East Coast, and I decided before I went that I'd have an affair with a woman. She was a striking, sensual woman, lesbian but not a dyke, and it was the best experience of my life. This woman was great. She made me feel so sensual, so wonderful. She was so complimentary of me, as a woman, as a sexual person. She was so creative, she was so . . . I adored her. We both did oral sex, but it grossed me out a bit. I was almost but not quite orgasmic. We still remain good friends, but I made a decision to leave her—I wasn't man-hating, didn't want a gay lifestyle, wanted to be heterosexual.

"Not long after, I began psychotherapy. We worked through my Oedipal thing, that maybe I was holding back because I was hung up on Father, and we also discovered I had a big fear of orgasm. I was afraid something would happen, like I was going to pee or lose control of my body functions, somehow embarrass myself. So my therapist said, 'Go home and learn how to masturbate, find out what it's like, and you'll be less afraid in your relationships.' I was scared to death, but I always took her greatly to heart, and went home and did what she said.

"Then I started seeing another man who became my live-in for a while. I was pretty hesitant about it, but then, once I began experiencing orgasm with him, I was a little disappointed. I had been expecting 'Poooow!' Ultra explosion from the inside out. Instead I learned I have jerky legs, and my body really twitches! But in time I learned my body's needs, a lot of clitoral touching, and I let my partners know it. My last few affairs have been very good, very intense and orgasmic."

Integrated with physical touch, Mimi employs a repertoire of mental stimulation: "I can see and do 'D: all of the above'! It may sound artificial or contrived, but it's really not. It's interesting, kind of creative for me. It's very easy to just go in and have a sexual experience, just screw, and I can do that, but there's an art to being sexual or sensual, and it's not simply taking your clothes off. There's a lot of mental work and attitude involved.

"I like experiencing fully in my life, and I don't like mediocre experiences. I like to bring sex out of the mundane and make it a thrill and exciting. You've got to be creative every day of your life. Energy begets energy. The more passionate you act, the more passionate you'll feel.

"I think of myself as the most adult whenever I'm making love. A very adult experience. I feel the most mature, the most womanly."

When easily orgasmic women actively use their minds to enhance the sexual experience, they are not mechanically applying "technique," but are, rather, creating an event of beauty and originality. They express their own personalities, their life experience and desires. Natalie, the woman who finally broke the bond that tied her to her mother, states the fact like this:

Fantasies of bondage, whippings, leather boots, chains —nothing about it bothers me other than 'That's not me.' I want to be in lace. I want to be in lingerie. I'm a big lingerie person, I buy a lot of it and I love it. In my fantasies, the men are very, very gentle and calm.

I'm a romantic, very much a romanticist. They're
doing what I want them to do because I'm controlling
what's happening. It's *my* fantasy.

And creative events are often spontaneous, arising without
conscious effort:

I don't make a decision ahead of time to go for a
fantasy or mood. I go with however I feel when I'm
there. If I close my eyes and James Taylor is
underneath the lids—he's there.

And Nora, the organized woman who started this chapter,
who learned to do it *her* way:

When a picture appears in my mind, like what I'm
doing while I'm making love, it's not a thought I seek
out. It might be there, or something might trigger it,
but it's not something I formulate. It's just a normal,
natural part of sharing the pleasures of love.

At last it's time to hold hands—but you may be surprised to
learn that, with easily orgasmic women, their sexual encounters
actually begin . . . long before fingertips brush.

# 4

# Starting on Warm

Before an evening when I'll probably make love, I'll try
a dress rehearsal in my mind. I know where I want to
get, the end result—in the bed under the covers, with
the little light on.
                                                    —*Rita*

Darcie is the woman who told of accepting her body; she
related part of her preparatory ritual in Chapter 2: "When
I'm going out, I want to look sensuous and sexy. Right then and
there I get a natural high and really begin to get into it.

"As I'm getting ready, I try to isolate myself in the bathroom
and bedroom. It's not always easy when the kids are there, but
I try, and on weekends they often sleep at my mother's. First
I wash my hair, then I take a nice bath. Usually I'm not thinking about sex yet, but I know that after my bath, after I get my
hair done, those thoughts will come.

"Then I close my bedroom door. I put music on, which is
very soothing, and it removes me from my everyday pattern.
It's a way of concentrating—you have to make the effort. I'm
standing before the mirror completely nude. I go through my
wardrobe and hold things up or try them on, how this view
looks, how that view looks. I'll take the bras . . . All of this is
arousing.

"I touch my body. I'm very sensitive on my breasts, my
nipples, so that all it takes is a little light touch to get myself
started. I don't usually masturbate before I go out—because I
wouldn't stop. I'd never make dinner at eight.

"As I'm dressing, I get myself excited. I have to go to the
bathroom several times. The anticipation grows. I have gone

through all the steps, established the mood before I even walk out the door, and it carries me through the evening. I'm ready for my sexual encounter."

For an easily orgasmic woman, the toilette can be a time of relaxation and isolation, of "focusing in" to lovemaking, of shedding the "outside world" and directing her thoughts and energies to the pleasures of making love.

She begins to get in touch with herself, her moods and desires, the ways of making love that she will find most arousing.

She begins to build her sexual confidence, and to sexually *arouse herself.* In effect, she begins to make love well before the physical encounter.

One woman stated, "I set myself up as irresistible with my grooming," and another always cleans her diaphragm and prepares her lingerie a day in advance of an expected encounter. And even younger women, including some who usually prefer spontaneity, instinctively understand the importance of preparation. This is a woman, age twenty-one, a university student:

"I don't consciously 'do' anything. But I know how I like to feel—what makes me feel more responsive. I never wear my glasses. I don't wear turtlenecks and sweaters like I do to classes. I sometimes wear low-cut shirts, or just silky things, skirts, and high-heeled shoes. It's not that I want to be more sexy, it's the femininity that I reach for. If I'm staying at my boyfriend's apartment, and I've been studying for two hours, I'll take a shower, wash and dry my hair, brush it, and put on one of his T-shirts, a short one, not a sexy nightgown. But it's still the feminine I reach for."

Kate, in her early thirties, is a sales representative for an office equipment manufacturer. She has short dark hair, and moves with the light, fluid strength of a dancer—which, for several years, she was.

"Growing up, I was active in church youth groups. Baptist,

very straight and fundamental. I married at twenty, and moved to Oklahoma. I was never very orgasmic with my husband. There were lots of things I wouldn't do, like oral sex, and I felt too guilty to explore—and I was just plain dumb. I never knew where my clitoris was until I was twenty-nine or thirty years old. I mean, I knew it felt good when I rubbed against him, or when I sat on my foot—that kind of thing—but that was about it.

"We split after ten years. I wasn't happy, and he found a girlfriend. That's when I went to Denver and worked as a dancer for a while. And I made a decision: 'Let's get this show on the road, Kate! You're not going to just sit here. You've got to do something with your life. You're still young. You've got to grow again!' And after that, learning has always been very important for me. I had just stopped, okay? I had children, I had a home, I had this, I had that—but I'd never stopped to do what was important for *me*. Then I went gangbusters to find out all I could."

Among many things, Kate learned how to be consistently orgasmic with a partner. "And I learned that I could have multiples, with oral sex, or if a penis strokes my vagina just right, along the side walls and slowly."

Kate takes special care with her grooming and bath: "When I'm going out, I pamper myself. I enjoy a change of dress from the normal everyday suit I wear to the office. The biggest thrill for me is when my children are sleeping out, and maybe it's a special occasion. I soak in the tub, and I light the candles and I take my wine in, and I do the whole bit. I scrub and perfume and touch myself from head to toe. I work myself over, and I exercise. I take pleasure in the feelings of my body.

"By the time my date picks me up, I feel so good about myself, even if he might not desire me—I desire me!"

Grace is the woman from a wealthy Eastern seaboard family, a nursing administrator who is married to a cardiologist: "Wednesdays, as well as the weekends of course, are special

54 ULTIMATE PLEASURE

because my husband rarely sees patients that day. I take time from my schedule—graduate school, job, my children—to always have my hair done differently. When I come home, I want to be isolated for a while, to relax in my sunken tub with only candles for light, and music over the intercom. The mood is relaxed and sensual. . . .

"I have a fragrance for every day and feeling, and all my soaps and bath oils match my perfumes. Depending on the mood I'm in, it's either a Bal à Versailles day or Tabu day or whatever. Each is special because my husband has picked every one; I never buy my own perfumes. And I love it, because by my selection I can tell where I'm at, and I think it cues it to him. Even the nightgowns. They're all designer gowns, tailored for me at a lingerie boutique, and I pick them out with the same care I give to my clothes, for the color and a special fit. I never buy nightgowns with buttons—buttons would drive me crazy —and I tend to like plunging necklines, gowns that are easily accessible. One is bolder than the other.

"In the bedroom there's music, sometimes a hot X-movie on tape, and a soft red light from the closet. . . ."

Several women prepare their PC muscles (the pubococcygeal or circumvaginal muscles that surround the middle third of the vagina) prior to a sexual encounter:

"Before I make love, when I go to the bathroom, I tend to prepare my PC's by stopping the flow off and on. It's excellent muscle exercise, and it's getting myself *ready*. Do you know how weightlifters go up, position themselves, do up their hands with rosin, and take a few blows, 'Whew! Wheh!'? Well, it's the same thing!"

And a few women in this study occasionally masturbate while still alone, before a probable sexual contact with a partner:

I occasionally bring myself to orgasm when I think I might not get there with a partner. Then I'm not hung up, and I'm more aroused and sensitive with him.

Now and then I touch myself before we make love. It makes me feel sexy and sensuous. And, with some subtlety, I let my husband know—he'll think about it driving home from the office.

Physical preparation for making love is a continuing enterprise. Many easily orgasmic women, aware of sexual fitness, as well as their general health and well-being, keep their bodies strong and limber. Others always keep their PC muscles toned, and a few, like Michelle, forty, the only widow in our study, cultivate sensuality as part of everyday life:

"I have noticed that certain fabrics I wear feel nice, and others feel uncomfortable—which sometimes can also feel good. I regularly find things with different textures and surfaces, and touch myself with them—my body, my breasts, my face. I close my eyes and *feel* them. I want to keep my sensitivity alive."

Dress serves several sexual purposes for easily orgasmic women. Besides alluring—or distancing—a partner, dress can help her express, fathom, or crystallize her mood. Iris, the former "rebel" who first had intercourse at twelve, says, "My black leather skirt and boots put me in a meaner mood. However I dress makes me feel that way, and most of the time that's the way I act. But in the summertime, I especially enjoy flowery and feminine things. I remember one morning when I went to a man's house, knowing that we'd make love, and I felt very summery with this flowy, light dress on—and nothing underneath. And a lot of times I like to dress in my leathers but wear very feminine lingerie—like saying 'Ah-hah! I fooled you!' "

Here are other comments on "everyday" dress, which the last woman calls "civilian clothes"—as opposed to those for sweet combat:

There are definite ways I can dress. If I don't want a sexual involvement with someone, I dress one way, and if I want an involvement, I dress another way.

When I'm going out on a date, I always know how I feel by the underwear I put on, and I favor open shirts and slim turtlenecks. If I *feel* sexy, it turns me on.

I dress for myself, to feel hot. My mood changes if I wear a garter belt, stockings, and heels to work—I feel sexy all day.

On a day-to-day basis, when the kids are around, and I can't dress exotically for sex roles, I wear certain civilian clothes that make me feel sexy and glamorous.

## Sexual Entertainment

Many of the women in this study enjoy—and are sexually aroused by—reading or viewing various kinds of erotica, either by themselves or in the company of a partner. Sometimes this reading or viewing takes place in the moments right before lovemaking. In the day or days preceding a sexual encounter, many of the women in this study read romantic fiction, which tends to foster amorous thought without supplying the details.

Several women enjoyed more explicit reading, publications such as *Playboy* or *Penthouse,* or sexually explicit stories that tickled their imaginations, or books specifically about sex. They particularly relished the pictures contained in these publications. A few women were pleased to have the publications available before or during a sexual encounter: "I associate myself with that sensual, naked woman." Not *any* naked woman, however; gross crudeness and extreme violence or sadism almost *always* is offensive, and a turnoff to a woman. Nevertheless, there are exceptions: "Roughness toward a woman turns me on, as long as it's not too heavy."

A greater number of women were aroused by "standard" movies and TV shows that contained romantic or sensual episodes or stories. And a substantial minority reported that they are sexually aroused by, and sometimes happily employ, pornographic or X-rated movies and video tapes: "It arouses me while I'm seeing it, enough that I feel myself lubricate." "When I see the movies, I imagine what they feel." However, reservations were frequent:

> I need a good story and mood to turn me on—and they're rare in pornography.

> I like soft, erotic films—never violence. A film of two women making love can arouse me—but I want a man.

> I enjoy some X-movies, but they get old, the excitement value gets "used up" quickly—though I still fantasize about some highly arousing scenes.

"Hot" media, such as movies and television, convey a sense of immediacy and vividness, and provide ready-made images. Yet women still use these images creatively, projecting themselves into the scenes and tailoring the script to their preferences. Nonetheless, more women prefer creating their own original visions.

Bernadette, now married, was raised near Chicago. A tall woman, almost six feet, she conveys a serene composure. She is an ex-nun: "When I was nineteen, my mother said to me, 'Go to the convent. Because if you get married, your husband will want to have intercourse.' I wore my habit until age twenty-four, but then I realized I did not have the vocation to be a nun —I wanted some kids and a husband." As for X-rated movies, Bernadette observes: "I like the movies occasionally, but they ruin my spontaneity, my own thoughts." She means, as we shall see, that more arousing images are in her imagination.

## Opening Communication

Communication about sexual intentions can begin far in advance of the physical encounter—with a letter, a telephone call, a glance.

"A lot of times, if I have to go somewhere, I'll leave him a little note. Sometimes I just say, 'Be ready tonight,' and perfume it, or leave a sheet from a prescription pad for the 'best medicine'—it has little pictures on it, of a man and woman making love. Or sometimes we'll mark our sexual position book, and leave it in the bathroom or on the bed. With a little note—'Try this tonight?' "

Such private messages allow a woman to anticipate the sexual encounter, to focus in on her desire and pre-arouse herself. The act of conveying *her own* intentions, and knowing that they contribute to her partner's excitement, is also highly arousing: "Sometimes I call him at work and say, 'I'm going to put the baby down for a long nap. Start thinking! I know you'll be ready by the time you get home.' I also know that dinner will be late that evening—we're having dessert first."

And another woman: "I usually don't wear underwear when I wear pantyhose. Sometimes when I feel romantic or sexy, I think about it. Depending who my date is, while we're dancing or at dinner, I might whisper to him: 'I've nothing on under my stockings.' He'll dream about that, and I'll think about how, later in the evening, it might be exciting for both of us."

Kate, the woman you met at the beginning of this chapter: "Eye contact is very expressive. If a person knows me, or has been around me enough, they know that my eyes tell a great deal. Or my body language. And I do little things—like in a car, a touch or a tease here and there. Showing a leg, or unbuttoning my blouse. I went with a man for two years who got a real kick out of things like this—and it stimulated me as much as it did him."

And Constance, the woman you met in Chapter 2, who once feared the feelings of orgasm: "Building my partner's anticipation makes me excited too. Sexy nightgowns, bikini underwear, a zipper that's almost all the way down to reflect enough without showing everything. You do that along with your eyes and body movements, a 'Come to me' attitude. . . ."

The above are all examples of more or less tacit or unspoken communications; sexual intention is conveyed with few, if any, words. But, naturally, conversation is most commonly used to open sexual communication.

Lovers, of course, can simply say, "Sweetheart, I love you. Let's make love." But sometimes the mood needs quickening. This is Ursula, the fifty-nine-year-old woman who was born on a farm in Kansas: "Before we make love, we have nice, light conversation that sets a mellow mood. Never anything deep, or involving problems. I make my husband believe he's the only male in the world. I tell him how great he is, how much I appreciate this or that. A little light kidding goes back and forth. And he thoroughly enjoys it when I compliment him—even if he's been grouchy that day. You have to lie a little."

The usual conversation is more overtly sexual—"sex talk":

I call and tell him I'm coming home to make mad, passionate love to him. Or tell him I'm going to do new and crazy things, so we both think about it. Talk is great before sex.

"Come up to the bedroom later. You can help me try on the new dresses I bought—and maybe even the underwear."

I love to talk about what we'll do sexually a day or so
in advance. Or I'll tell him about the new records I
bought, or how my bedroom is filled with fresh flowers.
Or one of us might say, "I bought some beautiful silk
ties the other day. What do you think we might do
with them?"

And touch. Making love, after all, eventually involves touching. What could be a better means of sexual communication?

No problem when he's watching a football game. I
simply go sit on his lap and squirm a bit.

We touch each other. I brush by him, or he pats me
on the ass or touches my boobs.

I hug or touch him physically to let him know.

When he comes home and touches me at the sink,
grabs my breasts from behind, I melt against him and
can hardly wait. . . .

I always try to touch a man in advance. It sets up a
"contact mood." Then I can better focus on my own
body and feelings.

## Preparatory Imaging

For easily orgasmic women, erotic mental activity usually
begins as part of their preparation for lovemaking.

In the past, this type of erotic mental activity has frequently
been treated as a single event, and has been termed "fantasy."
But mental activity is like music, or art—or life. All manner
and shading of "type" exist. Music varies from hard rock to
disco to romantic ballad to jazz to classical—to name just a few
variations. All are different in rhythm and mood, in timbre and

orchestration, in scope and depth, in force and complication. Yet all are music. Further, within each type are varieties: Chopin's nocturnes or Beethoven's Ninth Symphony—and, yes, even Ravel's *Bolero.* In any event, we intend to sort out a woman's mental music—but first, let's listen:

I build my thoughts and feelings, and think positive things about my husband.

I can intentionally do this before I go out—do a visual run-through of a book like *Lady Chatterley's Lover.* My intent is to heighten my feelings.

Sometimes, before I make love, I'll picture myself on the beach in the Bahamas, relaxed and warm. I try to recapture the tranquil atmosphere.

Occasionally I think about other men—sex with them —before making love with my husband. It arouses me for him. I visualize the scene, and that recalls the sensations. I get very moist. . . . I lubricate thinking about it.

I see an image of my husband and me, a past experience of making love in bed. And I usually get a physical sensation along with that thought.

*Natalie, the woman who prefers lace to chains in her fantasies:*
Hands are important to me. I can be sitting and talking with someone who has attractive hands— and get a flash image of his hands caressing my body.

*Mimi, the opera performer:*
   During the day, when I know I'll probably make love, I sometimes visualize what I'm going to be wearing that evening, and certain things that I'd like to

do. I rehearse it in my mind, so that I feel uninhibited when I actually do it. Or I make up my mind, "Mimi, you're going to do this," so that I don't back off from it.

*Meredith, the woman who demanded an hour to get in the mood, and then learned how to arouse herself in minutes:*
I regularly get this picture, both beforehand and while I'm making love. It's like a movie, and you see a lot of simultaneous shots all at once—all penises. They're sort of floating around, and then one comes into focus—and I *feel* it. It's not a "person," but there is that feeling, the sensation. And then there's motion to it, so you feel the rhythmic in and out . . . and all of this can be before he penetrates.

On occasion, when easily orgasmic women "think about" making love, days, hours, or minutes in advance of a sexual encounter, their thoughts can be *only* thoughts—vague feelings or ideas without specific mental words or pictures consciously attached. Usually, these thoughts are of a positive nature, and assist sexual pre-arousal by reinforcing the endearing or positive qualities of a partner or situation: "I review whether I trust the person, and then try to think positive thoughts about him."

However, most "thoughts" are actually *mental images,* or have the effect of producing mental images. As one woman states: "When I say 'thought,' I am always talking about mental pictures—my thought always creates them."

Most of us normally regard the occurrence of mental "images" as a visual experience. But mental images may also be *auditory,* recalling or imagining sounds and words, or *kinesthetic,* recalling or imagining touch, movement, feeling, or sensation. In this book, we describe the activity as *imaging.*

Preparatory imaging takes place before a woman has physical contact with a partner, or, in some instances, during the early phases of lovemaking.

A preparatory image need not be specifically sexual. Some are images of endearing, pleasant, or relaxing occasions that evoke a mood of pleasure, or a feeling of affection and love:

> I remember him when we went to St. Bart's on our honeymoon. I was sitting on the beach and looked up as he was walking toward me. God, he looked so good! I swear I'll be sixty years old and I'll remember him walking down that beach, brown and tan and gorgeous! It gets in your chest . . . it's your breath, like "Ah!"

Strong physical sensations are linked to the image; this woman also evokes similar sensations when she visualizes her husband affectionately playing with her treasured pet. She reports, however, that she never has visual images during physical lovemaking, only "thoughts" or kinesthetic images, keen recollections of past sensations.

Most commonly, preparatory images are thoroughly sexual in content. Visual images of past lovemaking are frequent. In some, the woman visualizes the partner with whom she is preparing to make love:

> I see past times with my husband, exciting times we made love—like at my parents' cottage by the lake, or when someone once walked in on us.

> I imagine a quick run-through of a whole past wonderful evening—my lover, seduction, the rest—and I'm really aroused by the time I get to the orgasm.

And other preparatory images represent a past lovemaking experience with a different partner:

> Sometimes a picture of past encounters, my best ones,
> just pop into my mind—they're not voluntarily willed.

This last phrase highlights the point that preparatory, and, for that matter, *all* images, are not always voluntarily sought by a woman—many just "pop into" mind.

We also use the term "fantasy," reserving it, however, for a specific type of image, one involving extended internal images of the woman herself and/or other persons engaging in some activity. The fantasy may be purely sexual (such as two naked bodies making love) or more romantic in nature, and it usually includes some features of the environment:

"If I really want to conjure up a fantasy, like when I watch a movie, I can project myself and my husband into the movie, and it's usually romanticism, not pure sexuality. We can act out the parts—and a movie can be very titillating. We also saw some X-movies at a porn night at the university, *Deep Throat* and *The Devil in Miss Jones* and *Behind the Green Door.* Admittedly, parts of the movies are weak and laughable—but I think they are pretty entertaining most of the time! Later, when I get home, or months later, I can project myself into the scenes, either before or while we're making love.

"And reading books. Even when they're not explicit, I can get very turned on by books. With books, I don't exactly project myself into the story. The book just arouses me, and then I can take it from there."

This quote is from Meredith. She is articulate, and extremely aware of her images, but we quoted her again to demonstrate another point. Many easily orgasmic women have a broad variety of imaging options available to them, and they choose from among their options to suit the situation and their changing preferences and moods.

Wendy, the woman who was helped by her key partner, Zarek, calls her preparatory fantasies "What If" pictures: "Sure, I have fantasies. I visualize a man's surprise when I start taking my clothes off, and the next scene is screwing on the couch or something. I'm sure men do the same thing, sort of picture 'What If.' "

In *Sexual Behavior in the Human Female,* Alfred Kinsey and his colleagues found that the "average" woman had fewer general sexual fantasies—those not necessarily connected to a sexual encounter—than did men. He speculated that this might contribute to the fact that males are usually more aroused "before the beginning of a sexual relationship and before they have made any physical contact with the female partner." In that research, Kinsey did not investigate mental activity during sexual relations.

We have found that *easily orgasmic* women, particularly during a sexual encounter, but also before it, experience a substantial—if not an enormous—amount of sexual "fantasy" or, more broadly, erotic mental activity. Of the sixty women in our study, fifty-six report that, at least sometimes, they consciously prepare for sexual encounters, either "physically" or mentally. Physical preparation, naturally, also generates mental arousal; when Darcie, Kate, or Grace prepare themselves and focus into the anticipated sexual experience, they are also creating mental stimulation. Interestingly, the four women who reported no conscious preparation for sexual encounters, described, at other stages of the interview, *preparatory images or thoughts.* The willingness to pre-arouse herself when she desires to do so may, in fact, be one of the characteristics that distinguishes an easily orgasmic woman from a less orgasmic woman.

A note of reservation. Two women mentioned that "planning too much" can "backfire," leading to disappointment and hurt should the sexual encounter fall short of their expectations. Several other women, although they prepared on occasion, stated that they much preferred spontaneity.

In any event, preparation for a sexual encounter, whether it be physical or mental, whether it fosters concentration or relaxation, whether it bolsters a woman's sexual confidence or stimulates her nearly to orgasm, serves one natural purpose: It allows a woman to begin her sexual encounters "on warm," enhancing the probabilities that she will enjoy the sexual experience, and be orgasmic with a partner.

## Dress Rehearsal

Many easily orgasmic women image a "run-through" of their anticipated sexual encounters.

Rita, in her early thirties, is an attractive woman from a family that "bordered" between Orthodox and Conservative Judaism. She is currently the head buyer for an important division of a department store. She has long auburn hair, and the lean, strong figure of a jock who regularly runs 10K's "to take up my aggression." She was born near Los Angeles.

"My mother used to think that when I'd go to a party with the boys in high school, that the lights would be on, that everyone would be dancing, and the mother would be serving hot dogs—my mom was 'Leave It to Beaver.' In reality, an older brother would go out and get us beer or Southern Comfort, and we'd go back to someone's house whose parents were out of town or not home, and we'd drink and make out. Part of me was doing what they expected of me, and part was doing what felt good."

Rita first had intercourse at the age of fourteen, experienced her first orgasm at nineteen, but was not consistently orgasmic until her late twenties. "I began to open up and explore my sexuality. And I began to masturbate more and more frequently —I was very determined to bring myself to orgasm because it felt so good. If I found out that standing on my left elbow would do wonders for me, I'd say to my partner, 'Hi, sweetheart, I've got something new I want to try.' "

Rita also began to prepare for her sexual encounters: "During the day I will have little fantasies about how we are going to make love. I will think, 'Well, how am I going to do or say this or that?' I'll try a dress rehearsal, what I'm going to say, what he's going to say, and by rehearsing, I know what it's going to take to get to the act.

"I will put myself in that mood. If it's going to be a very lustful thing, I'll put myself in a mood by what I'm wearing or how I'm acting. I can be bitchy, be a little girl, be Victorian, be whatever my mood is or how I want to respond sexually. I'll think about when or where, but I don't plan it—I think about it.

"I call my favorite role 'The Undercover Bitch.' The Undercover Bitch is like the secretary image with the nice skirt and her hair up in a nice little bun and glasses and her blouse buttoned to here, but then her glasses come off and her hair comes down and there's something inside—prim, proper, but sexy. Soft and feminine, but sexy—there's always that bit of sexiness in there. It's always happened anytime I want to feel it, and that's when I'm in control. Maybe not really in control, but in my *mind* I'm always in control. I know my mental attitude says that 'You are going to be the bitch, the naive one, the intellect,' and so I am confident because I've got it mentally, I've got it outwardly and inwardly, so I'm very confident that that image is going to be in control—that it is going to work.

"It's a confidence builder, a very confident sexual feeling. I feel good about myself because I'm comfortable in what I'm wearing. I'm comfortable in my train of thought, with the way the night might progress, that the end result will be—could very possibly be—that we'll end up in bed together, and I'm very pleased with that.

"If you're confident, you're not going to be as inhibited. Being confident is unhiding yourself, opening up. Because I'm picturing in my mind something I've *already experienced.* I know the feeling of an orgasm. I know the feeling of being uninhibited. I know the feeling of making love with the lights on. I know the feeling of exploring someone else's body. I know all those feelings. To visualize them, to know that I can do it and have done it, brings a feeling of confidence that I can do it again.

"With my partner, there's a time period prior to being in bed, the seduction. It starts with flirtation, the talking, the feeling each other out to get the approach. If I am not wildly attracted to or stimulated by that person, I still know that if I get myself in the mood, I will enjoy the sexual experience. So I get myself in the mood. I will be seductive. I will be coy. I will be bitchy. I will be flirtatious. But I will get myself in the mood.

"My physical attraction to a man depends on how orgasmic I am with him. Because I'm not going to not enjoy sex anymore. I'm going to enjoy it."

Rita images and rehearses a "role." She identifies her mood and the facet of her personality she wants to be. By preexperiencing a probable situation, she establishes sexual confidence in herself and enhances her sexual arousal.

Few of the women in this study rehearse their sexual encounters as extensively as does Rita. Yet role rehearsal or runthrough imaging is still the most prevalent form of preparatory imaging. About one-third of the women in this study sometimes experience a form of this type of imaging prior to a sexual encounter:

I develop a picture with dialogue and conversation. It transfers my mind to sex.

The more I think about it, the better it is. My mind goes through a seduction scenario, and I focus on sensations and feelings.

I plot how to seduce him—but I'm flexible. When we're making love, I go with my urges at the moment.

We might note that the seduction sequence is extremely important in preparatory run-throughs. In fact, many images are only of that, the seduction. Partners should be aware of this; some amount of seduction and preparation is always desirable —and sometimes necessary—in a satisfying sexual encounter.

And Kate. You might believe that teasing with a leg or unbuttoning her blouse is the extent of her seductiveness. Wrong.

"While we're having dinner or talking, I mentally undress him. I visualize what he looks like under his clothes, what he feels like, his skin. I'm trying him out.

"And suppose we've already been to dinner, and we've kissed, and I know I'm going to bed with him. Then it's my lead, and I visualize how it's going to be, how I will respond to him—whether I will go into the bedroom and slip on something nicely sexy, or something that looks totally perverted and kinky, or whether I will act innocent and let him undress me. And most of the time it works, I feel I have total control of the situation, and I understand what's going to happen. I can arouse myself. If the particular man is not enough to do it for me, then *I* do it for me."

Let us underscore the fact that Kate's preparation and love-making is neither mechanical nor calculating. She always assists her own arousal, yet she prefers the man to be "enough" to do it for her.

One woman tells of experiencing entirely auditory images ("The words come into my mind and I can actually *hear* them: 'I'm a strong, sexy black woman; I'm a strong, sexy black woman.' It helps me build myself up"), as well as images that symbolize her preferences and the sexual experience itself: "I think about flesh to flesh. As a matter of fact, I can see it now! I see two nude bodies, standing front to front, rubbing each other, caressing. That gets me in the mood and helps arouse me. In fact, I always see them when I think about sex. Touching is very important. For me, the best parts come before penetration. I guess that picture sort of means the pleasure of sex and touching."

And here are two last preparatory images, strongly linked with pleasurable and arousing sensations. Both are from Nora, the woman from the previous chapter who learned to make love *her* way:

"It's not a 'person.' I prefer the picture without a face that I know. It's like . . . if I were to close my eyes and just wait . . . for some mysterious hand to come out and touch me. I remember times when that picture has flashed in my mind, like a form of déjà vu, when I must be reminded of something. And, all by myself, I can get totally aroused by thinking how exciting it would be. It's not a fantasy because it's not like I try to pull in a face or situation. Sometimes I can place it, I can remember a sexual experience and put a face on it, but then I really prefer to block the face, because a specific person almost takes the feeling away."

"If I've made love the night before, but I didn't come because I've had too much to drink, or for whatever reason, usually, in the morning, I really want it. I'm focused on it, and I will start thinking about coming, the sensation and total excitement. Even if my partner's not quite awake, I want him to touch me and touch me *now*. I build, tell myself I'm excited—sometimes it's almost a little verbal—and think of how exciting it would be. I imagine that he just leans over and touches me, or the slightest thing, and then I get more detailed in my thoughts. I imagine him touching my clitoris, or putting his finger up me. . . . I'll just focus, and then if he merely touches my breasts— I go off like an alarm clock."

## *The Curtain Rises* . . .

Close to the sexual encounter, or during the early phases of lovemaking, many easily orgasmic women create an erotic environment.

They often desire a voluptuous or romantic atmosphere:

I like romantic moods, with sensuous, velvety materials. Candlelight and music, and taking a bath together.

When I know he's coming home shortly, I light candles and incense, and dress for him. We like negligees, and he likes me to wear black. When he hits the door, he knows I'm waiting.

I establish moods. We take a skinny-dip in our pool, then have some drinks by the fireplace. Firelight is lovely, and petting on the floor or sofa.

Sometimes preparations convey a hint or message:

If I'm in the mood for bondage, I leave my stockings lying on the chaise or bed.

I love nature, and making love outdoors, at the beach or in the woods. When I suggest we have a picnic or a walk by moonlight, and pack my little quilt, I'm sure he knows.

I set a provocative, seductive mood. I spread my fur coat on the bearskin rug—and I love to screw on both of them.

And, now and then, women who desire to act out a role or fantasy make sure that their favored accessories are ready and close at hand.

And finally, preparation—again, before physical contact or during the early stages of lovemaking—often includes erotic dress. Approximately half the women, on occasion or often, use frankly erotic, provocative dress to excite and seduce their partners—as well as to please themselves.

I do have pretty nightgowns, but something that shows cleanliness and softness is enough.

I answer the door in my lingerie.

I answer the door naked.

I love garter belts. His excitement arouses me.

Negligees, stockings, and garter belts—I love them. They make me feel sexy and feminine.

My wedding dress doesn't fit too well anymore—but it has sixty white buttons, all the way down. I don't like the "Hurry, take off the lingerie" thing. I like the slow taking off of things. . . .

I like stockings, heels, and garter belts. I have a skirt that's cut to the waist, and panties split up the middle. And *I* feel pleasure from wearing them. I like my appearance and the feel of satin. . . .

In touch with their moods, sexually confident, and *pre-aroused,* easily orgasmic women "start on warm" when they enter a sexual encounter.

And now the curtain rises . . . Within the sexual encounter, an easily orgasmic woman begins by paying attention.

# 5

# Focusing In

When I'm making love, it's like being in another world.
I completely block out everything everywhere except
right where I am at the moment. There's nothing in the
world but that room and that bed.

*—Vivian*

E*very* woman, bar none, agreed upon one subject in our
interviews—to be orgasmic with a partner, she needed to
"be there" mentally, to concentrate upon and focus in on lovemaking. They isolate lovemaking from the "outside world," so
that "nothing else exists" but the moment:

*Darcie:*
I say to myself, "I'm going to make love to him
tonight, and I'm going to erase everything else from
my mind that I possibly can." At that moment,
making love is something I want to do, and I think of
nothing but sex.

*Mimi:*
When I'm making love the rest of the world goes
bye-bye.

*Nora:*
When I'm about to have sex, I concentrate on the
situation, on getting myself psyched up for it, on
getting my lover excited and drawing him into my
mood.

*Wendy:*
I make a commitment when I'm with someone—even if

it's a quickie. I'm participating with this person, and
I'm going to be there.

And other women:

I close my eyes and feel my skin and nerves, and start
to concentrate on myself as a whole person.

Focus in on each other, and only on making love.
Create a separate world.

Concentrate. A positive, relaxed attitude works
wonders.

*Relaxation* is often a necessary precursor to concentration.
Some women can make a quick transition from everyday bustle
to lovemaking, but most need time to "regroup," to distance
themselves from the outside world before they are able to concentrate.

Ginger is twenty-one, a strawberry blonde with long curly
hair and lively, cool green eyes. She is the mother of two children, a gregarious conversationalist, and an ambitious sales-
woman who intends to own her own business someday:

"If I've had a tough day at work, I'm just not prepared for
orgasm. When we're going to make love, I have to get away
from the kids and the house. Usually I just lie down and relax.
I block the kid stuff from my mind, stretch my whole body, then
think of my body parts, progressively relaxing each one. A bath
is good, then talking to my husband to establish some intimacy.
Our time together is limited, so we have to focus in on each
other, give quality time. If I can have just ten minutes a day like
that, to relax, maybe smoke a cigarette or have a glass of wine,
then everything is fine for an orgasm. . . ."

By relaxing, a woman clears away mental clutter, obtaining
space in her conscious mind for arousing erotic stimuli. She
turns her mental energy to sex, shedding fatigue and tension
through rest, a bath, a massage, or exercise. Then she refreshes

her strength, gets in touch with her body, and readies herself to build and receive the sensations of pleasurable *sexual* tension.

Some women, before making love, create an inner mental state perhaps best described as "serenity."

Eve, in her early twenties and single, works as a waitress to support herself while finishing her college education. She is winsome, athletic, enthusiastic, and projects a sweet but determined disposition. While she's making love, Eve makes a conscious effort to concentrate on the moment: "I usually don't think of anything except what I'm doing. I'm thinking of my partner, his responses, my responses. If I find I'm not getting excited because my mind's not in it, I try to think about sex or touching or getting turned on—I bring myself back to the moment. I may, on rare occasions, flash back to a scene that I liked in an X-rated movie, but I usually think of being with my partner, how much I love touching him. Or I may look at his penis and think, 'Oh my God, this is fantastic! This is really turning me on. That's really sexy, I'm getting excited!' I get myself excited with my mind."

During physical contact with a partner, Eve rarely experiences visual images; instead, she prefers auditory stimulation, and focusing her mind on sensation. However, before or during the early phases of lovemaking, she often experiences what she calls "relaxation fantasies": "One of my favorite fantasies is a vision of myself running free through a field. I'm barefoot, with a long dress on, my dress and hair trailing behind in a breeze. Then I'm 'rescued' by a knight in shining armor—he's on horseback, of course. A handsome prince just sweeps me off my feet and takes me away on his horse. Or sometimes I have him get off the horse and run with me through the field, or have us make love in the grass, quietly, gently, at peace. . . ."

And another woman frequently employs a different type of serenity image: "I learned this from a woman who is a psychic, and I use it often, sometimes just to relax and sometimes before

I have sex. The scene, each detail, is always precisely the same. I am alone, and I visualize myself walking in a wooded area, down a path and steps to a cottage. The steps are formed from railroad ties, and the path is bordered by African violets, rhododendrons, and hills-of-snow, all in bloom, and I always notice the plant pots and even nails in the cottage wood. Inside I sit on a bench. I can summon someone to talk with, about anything that's bothering me, or sit alone and meditate until my body feels calmed. Then I leave, retracing my steps, noticing each detail again, everything pleasant and calm. . . ."

Relaxation is also a theme in the use of alcohol and street drugs, which the women in this study basically limit to cocaine and marijuana. Most of the women, though, avoid excessive— or any—use of these substances and, so far as we could determine, no woman had ever been addicted to any chemical substance. Of those women who have used them, a few report novel or heightened sexual effects, or mild disinhibition, but no woman stated that any of these substances helped her become orgasmic. A majority of the women who did use these substances, usually alcohol and in moderate amounts, stated that their normal intent was to foster relaxation—to focus in more effectively and concentrate on sex.

However, every woman who had used *any* of these substances emphasizes that excessive use can easily render her *non*-orgasmic and, perhaps more important, disrupt the flowing give-and-take of relationship with her partner. She may dull her senses, "get sloppy," lose concentration and energy, lose control of her muscles—and lose awareness of sharing. Generally, the women in this study desire to "be there" with an alert mind, to focus upon sensuality with a responsive body, and to fully participate in the sexual and interpersonal—not drug—experience with a partner.

## *Eliminating Distraction*

As she prepares for her sexual encounter and relaxes before making love, a woman slowly narrows her focus to none but the pleasure at hand, until, during lovemaking, nothing exists but the instant. Yet any woman can be distracted while she is making love. The telephone rings, a child wails from his crib, vagrant thoughts infiltrate her mind—a job assignment hangs incomplete, a car requires repairing, her checkbook refuses to tally with her bank statement. Or negative thoughts concerning her partner suddenly come to mind—she thinks of his short-comings, or is reminded of past conflicts or annoyances with him. Or sex, for the moment, seems tedious, and her mind is a wandering blank.

The women in this study actively deal with such distractions. To enjoy the lovemaking moment, and to be orgasmic within it, each woman knows she must rid her mind of all but erotic thoughts, and many employ specific techniques to ensure that they are focused on love.

Before they begin making love, many women clear the physical environment. They ascertain that their children are cared for, or otherwise "warned away"; the bedroom door is locked; the phone is removed from the hook. Sometimes, of course, these efforts are fruitless—it's daytime and young ones are running about, a child or relative is ill or in trouble, a business call is expected. Nevertheless, whenever possible, the women secure or "exclude" their environment, and concentrate on sex. Several women, recognizing their compulsive bent, not only clear the environment but make sure that it's carefully ordered: "I wouldn't advise leaving something in the oven!" "I clean the room—sometimes the whole apartment—and get my work in order. Then I can concentrate better—in fact I *feel* better."

Yet, no matter how ordered or untidy her environment, a woman must clear her mental clutter before she can truly savor lovemaking with her partner. When foreign thoughts intrude, the most common strategy, consciously employed by two-thirds of the women, is to "concentrate more" on lovemaking, to "just block out" distraction. This is Nora's comment:

> Sex is one of the finest times of my day. Even though I know I have to get somewhere or I have to prepare something, whether it's for five minutes or an hour, all my worries are gone—whoosh, they're just wiped out. So I just block out distractions.

Another woman:

> This is *our* time. I shut distraction out, make up my mind that I'm going to concentrate on what I'm doing. Sex is the only aspect of our relationship that we don't have to share with anybody. With four kids from two different families, ex-spouses and ex-in-laws, there's just so much of myself and my relationship that's constantly up for grabs. So, when we're making love, the rest of the world's just going to have to go pound salt. Nobody and nothing's going to interfere with *my time!* I shut *everything* out.

And others:

> Concentrate, snap it out of your mind, let your cares go—mind over matter. Enjoy the moment.

> I will other thoughts away, tell my mind to stop and erase them.

> I tell myself, "Nothing is so important, take care of other things later. Enjoy this."

Many women block distraction by becoming more sexually active. Lisa, the woman you met in Chapter 3 who wants to be a TV reporter, makes this observation:

Every now and then something distracting creeps in. First I'm thinking, "God, this feels good," then my mind takes off and I think, "My God, what am I doing thinking about the laundry!" I immediately put myself back into sex, usually by getting more active. I've noticed that when my mind trails, it's when I'm not being active.

Other women agree, or seek to block distraction by focusing on sensations:

I try to do something aggressive, to take the assertive role.

If I'm in a passive role, and a noise or a thought distracts me, I concentrate on my physical sensations and take an aggressive role. I have to be physically active to block things out of my mind.

I put distractions out of my mind and go back to what I'm doing. I usually hunt for pleasurable sensations and concentrate on them—a deliberate thought of what feels good.

A substantial number of women, some 20 percent, invoke fantasy or other images to counter unwanted thoughts. As Natalie states it, "I change the subject." Iris counters a wandering mind with fantasies of anal sex or making love with a stranger. Other women:

Sex is both a need and an escape, so you don't start dragging in everything else at that particular time. If

something mentally intrudes, I just start thinking about
my visual pictures.

I tell myself that this is my time and I'm just not
going to think about things. Then I usually put myself
in a fantasy.

A few women "go with" extraneous thoughts, letting them
run their course, and a few others "talk out" distractions with
partners, then resume making love. And, of course, on occasion, a woman can be so distracted—sometimes by truly important events—that she knows it's best to not make love at
all.

## Concentrating Through Shortcomings and Conflicts

A single woman without a steady relationship still has sexual
needs and desires. At any given moment she may wish to share
and enjoy her sexuality or, like several women in our study,
prefer a brief or extended period of deliberate celibacy. But
there is always a first time with a partner—and little surprises
await us in the universe. No matter how long we "know"
someone, lovemaking, that ultimate, intimate moment, reveals
a new depth of knowledge, both about our partner and about
our emotions and values concerning him or her.

A woman may find herself in a very human situation. The
man may be either a virtual stranger or only a casual friend, and
she discovers, subjectively, while making love, that she desires
no deeper intimacy. She may encounter a physical turnoff (an
uncircumcised penis perhaps, or callused, clumsy hands) that
for her, as an individual, disrupts her concentration. Or the
man may be inexperienced or seem inept as a lover. In any
event, now and then during lovemaking, a partner's minor
shortcoming will leap to her conscious mind. We asked the
women how—or if—they dealt with such situations, and

whether they were orgasmic despite such minor flaws. We guessed that if a woman was able to be orgasmic under somewhat adverse conditions, she might offer valuable clues to less orgasmic women.

When this eventuality arose, and it often did, the vast majority of women in this study were able to be orgasmic. Generally, they used strategies similar to those that helped them cope with mundane distractions, adapting them to the situation. For example, many women merely block "undesirable aspects" from their minds, become more sexually active or "dominant," or concentrate on their own sensations.

Positive words and thoughts take on a slightly new flavor:

I tell myself "So what?" and compare it to a past experience where my partner wasn't perfect and everything worked out fine.

I think, "This is for me, my benefit," and I try to appreciate the person by dwelling on his good points.

If I'm half aroused, I get into him as a person and find something I like—maybe he's touching me softly. Or I tell myself, "He was just with the wrong women before, and I'm not perfect either."

Several women consciously "maneuver around" a fault—they steer the conversation toward a partner's erotic strengths, or think only of positive parts of a partner's body and face, or limit their sexual activities to those that finesse the flaw. And several women deal with the problem through imaging, or by mentally endowing their partner with superior qualities:

I imagine the great times I've had with other men, or go to my favorite lesbian fantasies.

When my partner is not as desirable as I'd like, I work a bit harder with my mind. I can put another face on

him, or make him a body-builder. Of course, I
much prefer him a perfect ten—then we just get into
it.

When a woman is married, or involved in a steady relationship, another type of distraction all too frequently rises. Relationship is paramount. Few, if any, of the women in this study
can divorce "pure" sexuality from emotional feelings for a long-
term partner. But how does a woman make love when the
minor annoyances and conflicts that arise in any long-term
relationship undermine her desire for sexual pleasure and intimacy? Moreover, how does a woman *enjoy* lovemaking, to the
point of being orgasmic, when reminded of these conflicts while
making love with her partner?

Naturally, severe conflicts are always disruptive to lovemaking, and can smother a couple's sexual desires for long periods
of time. Here we wish only to discuss ways of overcoming
mental distraction from "minor" or "moderate" conflicts.
Every woman had experienced the problem, and each knew
how she dealt with it.

Some 10 percent of the women do not make love if conflict
escalates beyond the petty level: "I don't make love if I'm
upset." "There was too much conflict in my marriage. Now I
avoid sex if that situation happens." A smaller group, some 5
percent, often make love anyway, but usually are nonorgasmic
at these times. The remaining women, the vast majority, use
techniques to overcome strife and focus in on lovemaking, usually obtaining orgasm.

When thoughts of conflict arise during lovemaking, many
women stop making love in order to "talk out" the problem: "If
it's really bothering me, I talk about it right then, and it's
usually gone by the time we make love again." "Stop and talk
it out. I continue if our talk goes okay." However, a substantial
number of women simply set aside thoughts of conflict, and
deal with them later:

Block it out, enjoy the moment, and think tomorrow's tomorrow.

I tell myself it can wait, then set it aside to deal with later—best is another day.

Push it aside and concentrate—voicing arguments will only turn you both off.

In addition, most women turn to the strategies used to ward off mundane thoughts—they become more sexually active, tune in to their bodies and sensation, or conjure up a fantasy. Or they turn their thoughts to the positive:

Have a little talk with yourself—"It's over, we made up, this is fun. Enjoy what you're doing now."

I tell myself, "Accept him and his quirks—that's just him."

One of my biggest things is to think, "Well, this is my husband, he wants to make love to me, and that's really wonderful."

Meredith says, "Sometimes when we're not 'with it,' we go ahead and make love, but it's very dissatisfying. I can be orgasmic, my thoughts will leave me for those fleeting moments, but it won't be intense or as good.

"So what I've learned to do sometimes is visualize a blackboard in my head, and just erase everything on it. Everything distracting me is already written there, and I see myself erase the list until the blackboard's clean. When you're making love is not a good time to have discussions, serious or even minor —they just get out of proportion. So, if I'm already making love and something comes into my mind, it will be on the blackboard and I'll erase it, consciously try to shed it."

Other women make similar lists to help them concentrate on lovemaking. Here are two variations:

To orgasm, to be in the present, I really must put other thoughts aside, but feelings about my relationships sometimes intrude in my mind. When that happens during lovemaking, I think of the nice things I share with my partner, but often, beforehand, I'll sit down and write a list of my problems, and put the list in a drawer—off my mind and out of the way.

I'm a union steward, and I used to bring everything home from work—I'd be a real bitch for the evening. You know, "Don't touch me, don't come near me, leave me alone." My husband and I weren't getting along, and I had real problems with orgasms. Then I decided to put a mental block in, leave things at work. Here's how I do it: In my mind there's a little suitcase, and in go my problems, one by one. The suitcase goes up in my locker, and stays there until I come back the next morning. There it goes! I do that a lot.

Of course, a number of women felt that lovemaking helped resolve problems, or that conflict could even add zest:

*Ursula:*
Making love is a good way to get over an argument, to heal it.

*Constance:*
Some emotion is good. Sometimes I'm more aroused and aggressive, with a little more energy to sex.

*Mimi:*
When I'm angry or upset with someone, I want to get back to physical closeness and contact.

*And Nora:*
I suppose that arguments afford an opportunity to
straighten things out, to get back together. But I'm not
an argumentative type, and I don't usually argue or
fight with my partner. I never have. A lot of times,
after being mad or upset about something, I'll just turn
to face him while we're talking and slowly take off my
clothes, and then say, "Let's go to bed."

There is an "ultimate" kind of focusing in. A few women
relax so fully, eliminate distraction so completely, then concentrate so intently, that now and then their mental state resembles
a hypnotic trance. Vivian's quote begins this chapter; you met
her in Chapter 1, the woman who needed twenty-eight years to
become consistently orgasmic. She prefers spontaneous lovemaking and, aside from an occasional preparatory image, reports a minimum of preparation—yet once she's making love,
her concentration is total. In fact, her "trance" or immersion
is so rapid and complete that she can be orgasmic through
primarily hypnotic suggestion.

"I have complete faith in John, my lover. Perhaps it's a form
of self-hypnosis, but it always takes his voice to arouse me. His
voice is wonderful, deep and reassuring.

"But anyway, there we are, driving along a highway maybe.
Perhaps I'm a trifle drowsy, and sometimes he places his hand
on my leg. 'Darling,' he might say, 'do you see that bridge far
ahead? When we pass under it, you will have an orgasm.' He
continues to talk while we drive, and sometimes I giggle when
I feel it happening. I focus my eyes on the bridge. Then I just
feel the sensations, aware of my body and the heat inside, like
everything down there is throbbing. Sometimes I really let go
and move, so if we pass a truck—this can get embarrassing—
I shut my eyes until it's gone, then stare again at the bridge.
'Here comes the bridge,' he whispers. It's coming . . . we pass
under . . . I come. . . .

"I don't really know how I do it! I just relax and let it happen, take everything else out of my mind. I just . . . at that moment, that's the only place I am.

"I can do it at the breakfast table in the morning, or when we're flying alone in his private plane. Afterwards, I'm usually sleepy. . . ."

We might note that, along with her deep concentration and the erotic stimulation of her lover's voice, Vivian is usually sleepy and relaxed—and therefore open to hypnotic suggestion —before these episodes happen. She is immersed in, and sensitive to, every nuance of her internal sensations, and through slight or substantial movement, she also undoubtedly provides herself with physical, genital stimulation.

Nonetheless, her experience underscores the very heart of this chapter: To obtain orgasm, easily orgasmic women totally focus on the moment—lovemaking—and eliminate, as much as is humanly possible, all physical and mental distraction.

And now, as Nora suggested, "let's go to bed"—and explore the sensual pleasures of bodies in motion.

# Building Toward Orgasm: Physical Desires    6

> Today, men are focused on your clitoris, like, "Oh God, look! I found the magic spot!" But wait a minute, boys, there's still a lot of territory out here and it's all connected!
>
> —*Coral*

Sex can be a transcendent experience of communion between two lovers, but sex is also an earthly joy, replete with luscious sensations. In the soft, sensual crucible of sexual interaction, a woman gives and gains the heights of physical pleasure.

On one level, sexual arousal and orgasm are natural, wild, and simple; on another level, both are immensely complex. For clarity, we have divided the chapters on lovemaking into chapters describing primarily "physical" aspects, and a chapter describing primarily "mental" aspects. In life there is no such distinction. A woman's body and mind are one, and, at orgasm —perhaps as a *prerequisite* to orgasm—the two are exquisitely blended.

## Square One: Communication

When a lover hasn't the foggiest notion whether he's irking or pleasing, has no idea of a woman's tastes, her state of arousal, or her sexual needs, delightful love is improbable—and her orgasm merely a dream. As one woman stated, "Without communication, why *have* a partner?"

Nearly every woman emphasizes that communication tops

the list on "How to Be More Orgasmic" when making love with a partner:

Essential. How will he know if you don't tell him? Don't sit around feeling sorry for yourself—speak out!

Even if he's a husband, we can't lay it all on a man and give him the burden of making this a satisfying experience *we're* having. A woman should communicate with her lover—if you don't say anything, he thinks what he's doing is satisfying you.

I'm slower to reach orgasm, and if I didn't communicate the pace, but let him set it, I'd probably get left behind. And I'm usually not aware of what I'd like until I'm into it. How is he to know?

I've found that seventy-five to eighty percent of my partners can follow my responses—and sometimes he's close but missing. Men wait for some sort of communication.

I wasn't orgasmic for ten years—and only because I didn't tell lovers, when they found exciting sensations, to *keep on going.* Now, by communication, I've molded my husband to please me.

It's important to be open. Only you know your body. Indicate what works or doesn't, either verbally or physically. Communication is sharing the experience, to make it lovely for both of you.

A few responses were qualified. Some women felt that familiarity, or the intuition of lovers, could make verbal messages unnecessary: "He knows." "Better partners seem to sense what to do." And some thought too much "instructing" could spoil the thrill of novelty: "It's important, yes—but not always.

There's excitement in the unknown, in not knowing if he'll find it, not knowing what he'll do next."

## *Verbal Communication*

Some women use the direct verbal approach to convey specific needs or desires:

> To be orgasmic with intercourse, I also need him to touch me with his hand, to get more clitoral sensation, and the only way to be sure he knows is to tell him in so many words.

> I love nipple stimulation, harder at orgasm, and I have to tell that to a lover.

> I don't think there's anything wrong with telling a man what to do. After all, it's your body; you know where it's pleasurable, and he doesn't. Especially for oral sex, where it's sometimes hard to find a spot that really feels good—and where his tongue isn't stretched out ten inches.

Yet cautions abound. Fully 25 percent of the women offered warnings, advice, or tried-and-true methods for direct sexual communication. Most hints involved the male ego:

> *Nora:*
> Somehow, you must tell your partner how you can come, but men can be very sensitive to verbal suggestions. Be aware of a man's ego.

> *Erica:*
> Try soft verbal pleas, like "Lick me, oh please lick me," but don't set up demands, like "Do this" or "Don't do that."

*Ginger:*
I don't like to interrupt the spontaneity, so we talk a
lot *afterwards.* Men take suggestions harder than
women, as if it's criticism.

*Wendy:*
Women have to let men know what they want—which
is hard. You're always afraid of threatening a man if
you don't like how he's touching you, or if he's
touching you in the wrong place. It's so strange—like
we're telling them their business!

Some women, like Michelle, the widow who cultivates touch
sensitivity, can talk about their expectations before they go to
bed: "I sometimes say, 'If we're going to go this far, if we're
going to bed, then we both should have gratification. That's the
way it's supposed to be. I have these feelings, I have these
desires, and if you're finished and I'm left hanging, I expect
some help.' " But Michelle hastens to add: "Be careful. If you
lay it on too much, men will doubt their capabilities, and sometimes they can't perform." Her advice also pertains to ongoing
talk during sex: "With most of my partners, I find if I get
suggestive, with requests or things like, 'Could you do that a
little harder?' that it sets them back a little. Then I have to start
over again because they lose their concentration. So, if I can get
to them with a gesture or a touch or a movement, I try that
first."

Some particularly experienced women use indirect suggestion:

I try to explain my fantasies beforehand, and hope he'll
get the message.

Sometimes before, or while we're making love, I'll
demurely ask him questions: "Have you tried this . . . ?
Do you like that . . . ?"

I'm finding out that communicating has a hell of a lot
to do with becoming a woman. You don't use dry
words—"This is what I like and don't like"—but a
little seductive suggestion. Like, "If you kiss the back
of my shoulder, I'll go out of my mind. So please don't
do anything like *that!*"

Or soft, seductive tones:

Never be shrill or demanding. Use a soft, slow,
provocative voice.

Or cries of delirious passion:

"Ah . . . ! You're fucking me beautifully!"

"Harder, faster . . . !"

". . . deeper, stronger!"

"This feeling right now is marvelous! Keep going . . .
ahh!"

"Wow, that feels fabulous, please keep doing what
you're doing."

"I'm ready!"

"That feels marvelous, fabulous! Don't
stop!"

You might say these words are also slightly (!) encouraging.
Coral keenly appreciates this approach. Divorced, the mother
of six children, she is a registered nurse who is working for her
doctorate in psychology—to become a sex therapist: "New
partners usually explore all over so that when they hit, you
know, it's like shaping behavior. It's disgusting to be educated!
I give him positive reinforcement, the Skinnerian technique!

And when he stumbles on a stimulation I love, I say, 'Hah! Oooh! That's utterly marvelous!' "

### Body and Sound

Many women are naturally shy or feel uncomfortable when speaking of sex, and even a normally candid woman can be in a situation where words are inappropriate:

I find it hard to ask for things for myself. I'm just not good at it—particularly while making love.

I need to feel comfortable to say what I like, and it's not easy with a new partner.

Too many words are a problem—I want my husband to feel that everything is right.

I like a pinky up my tush at orgasm. Try telling *that* to a new lover.

And so you may find, as did the majority of the women, that *non-verbal* signs become your favored means of sexual communication. The body has limitless possibilities:

I do it by body cues, the way I wiggle and move.

I communicate rhythm with my PC muscles.

Body language, gestures, a soft quick touch tell him how he can have me.

I position myself, depending on whether I want intercourse or oral, and little moves tell him intensity.

If I touch my breasts, he's going to go for my breasts. If I reach down to my clitoris, he's going to take over there. They're *cues,* lover!

Some women have discovered a variation of this last technique—that what they do to a lover suggests their own desires, that he should do the same to them or try a similar pleasure. And others are more direct in signaling their desires:

I put his hand on my breast and slowly shift his body to where I want and need it.

When I want more clitoral feeling, I move his cock on my clit with my hand, or slide his hand to my pussy, guiding him with my fingers.

When I'm dying for oral sex, I move his head down my body.

And, finally, there is sound. Purrs, moans, and ecstatic cries are natural human responses to joyous sexual pleasure. They also communicate:

I'm telling him something when my cries escalate near orgasm.

I'm louder when it's good, sighs and groans, cries and screams—he knows when I'm going under.

It's not a "conscious" technique, but a natural response when it's heavenly. But I'm quieter when it's not.

Goodness! If you don't make noises, it's like two dead bodies lying there!

Of course, any of these methods or cues have their limitations. It requires patience and practice for lovers to know each other. Tracy, the woman you met in Chapter 1, who found her first intercourse beautiful, comments, "It's very hard to teach someone clitoral stimulation because it's kind of a moving hot spot. It's not always where he thinks it is, in the same spot, and you've got to know one another's bodies before it's really electric."

Uninhibited, long-term lovers develop intuitive communication, but they also use these specific techniques to enhance their sexual experience. Try them out or invent your own, choosing only those with which you feel comfortable. But never forget that your natural gifts—empathy, tenderness, caring rapport—will help you become more orgasmic if you give them a chance.

## *The Active—and Actively Passive—Woman*

You remember Constance—she became quite a partner: "Right in the middle of having intercourse I will physically place my hands on their shoulders, if they're on top, and push them off. Or I'll stop and tell them that's enough. I'll stop and I'll change it all around and go to oral or what have you—I love to keep things different, a variety happening.

"I say, 'More of this, harder, gently. Don't stop, don't stop.' And I moan and I groan, I always did, and they can read—I body-response to everything.

"I like to moan and groan. Scream sometimes. I won't scratch, but I do bite. Not hard, I don't leave any marks—I nibble. I caress them anally, often inside, usually with my finger or tongue. I enjoy it myself—and they respond. The quiet ones are going to moan and groan—no doubt about it. The quiet men always talk then!"

Not every woman makes love with the verve displayed by Constance, but easily orgasmic women are usually spiritedly active. An active sexual role has obvious physical advantages: "I control the positions and therefore the pace." "I set my own pelvic rhythm." "I want to be in control, on top, and get myself off by rubbing." Yet whether a woman tends to be active, passive-receptive, or somewhere in between, her choice of approach is a matter of taste, of partner and place, of mood and ease. No woman need be a sexual gymnast, but she needs to freely express *herself.*

Many orgasmic women take the sexual initiative:

> Initiative? Look, the first time I screwed my husband-to-be, I took him to a farm, out in the boondocks at midnight, and made it damn hard to resist me.

> I'm both forward and daring—and need to incite my husband to be more experimental.

> I tend to make the first move, set the tone and the rules.

> The first time I said, "I'd like you to tie me up," he said, "Oh no, I couldn't do *that.*" In the meantime he'd been telling me he couldn't do this and he couldn't do that and he couldn't—and then he did everything!

Though many women enjoy an aggressive role, often to the point of dominance, the best of all possible worlds is a match of affectionate equals. Iris: "Wimps bring out my dominance, but I go for aggressive men. They make me feel lovable and I like to cuddle—which I don't get a lot of because I'm such an aggressive woman, it's hard to find a man who is more aggressive than me. There's a conflict, because I want the affection and I want to be loved and I want to be cuddled—yet I want the aggressiveness. With a lot of men it's one or the other, but it's never both. And I want both. I have to have both, I have to!" She pounds the table and roars with laughter—"I have to, damn it!"

For other women, also, the byword is mutuality:

> I like to be active and dominant. Even if I'm in bondage, I want my hands free. Going back and forth

is best—I love to control and massage and kiss every inch of his body.

We both suggest impromptu ideas and we both love sixty-nine. When he teases the tip of my clitoris, I tongue inside his urethra or tease the tip of his glans— an almost compelling urge to respond to what he's doing.

Many active women, who want an equally active lover, fear threatening the man. Rita, who likes to think of herself as an "Undercover Bitch," observes: "Sex is one area where I'm extremely aggressive. Even when I'm coy, I somehow tell a man what to do. I know what I want, and some of that sexual aggression has a tendency to turn men off. So when I find a man to be aggressive with, and he is aggressive back, it works to really stimulate the sexual relationship."

Other women:

I like to be aggressive and in control, but in a fifty-fifty relationship. I'm attracted to men who can accept me as half dominant.

I like to be aggressive and dominant—*if* a man can handle it.

I get tired of doing everything. And I'm hesitant because I've threatened too many lovers. Sometimes I feel I'm too much for them, in every respect and sexually. I like a man to take the initiative.

A substantial number of vital women wished that men would be more aggressive and meet their end of the sharing. This doesn't mean that women desire force, excessive macho or selfish indulgence; they simply want their men to initiate more, invent excitement, make love with ardor. When her lover catches fire, a naturally active woman can also be more orgasmic: "I tend to do everything, take the positions, do the talking —whatever I feel the situation calls for. But I have been totally passive on occasion because I've wanted to be—and because my lover takes over. And I'm more orgasmic, much more if I don't have to think about anything—my lover is doing everything and it's just me there enjoying it."

Which brings us to the "actively passive" woman, who, though she wants to be passive, does not leave it to chance. She might indirectly persuade or provoke a man to be sexually aggressive, and a few actively passive women feel that they're secretly calling the tune: "At heart, a man really wants direction, to let me decide how to do it. So I'm there for the taking; I wiggle and squirm and moan, and make my body available— in ways I want to make love."

But for Vivian, nothing is more delightful than being caught unaware: "My favorite way to be turned on is when he's completely making the decisions about what he's going to do. I love it when I don't know it's coming and he takes me in the bedroom, throws me on the bed, takes my clothes off, passionately kisses me, then works his way down my body. . . . That's the ultimate."

## Building Sensation

Making love is sharing, and lovers delight in the feelings of joy experienced by the other. In the interplay of excitement there is no clear division of pleasure, but there are moments when one or the other takes or is given erotic stage center. And easily orgasmic women make sure of their limelight moments —when a man focuses his energies on giving her sexual pleasure.

Though pleasures interweave, the focus of this book is a woman's pleasure. In any case, even in research devoted equally to the sexual enjoyment of women and men, it is likely that greater attention would be accorded to a woman's gratification. Sexually, there is "more" of her, a more intricate system—her whole erogenous body, her extensive genital network, genital variations, her mind, particularly her emotions. Usually, she is slower than a man to become sexually aroused, and, ideally, more actual lovemaking time is expended upon her pleasure. And, once thoroughly aroused, she has a greater orgasmic capacity than a man, the potential, bestowed by nature, to reach a climax more quickly again.

We do not intend to provide a "sex manual." We do intend to elucidate the physical (and later, the mental) stimulations that a woman uses to build her sensations toward the peak of orgasm. As we speak of physical lovemaking, try to recall the rich and varied atmospheres two lovers can create—carefree, robust, spiritual, or steeped with erotic sensation. Use your imagination—and every one of your senses. Love is surrounded by sight and sound, fragrance and taste, and always touch. "You feel everything," one woman told us. "The whole body is erotic, and a lot of men don't know that." Women do.

When a woman communicates her sexual needs, and cues in her partner to her ongoing state of arousal, it's little to ask in return that he be a considerate lover. Even when she "starts on warm"—and even when she's easily orgasmic—a woman wants time for romantic affection and foreplay, and to make herself ready for orgasm. And, for a number of women, "foreplay," manual or oral stimulation, is one of the best parts of lovemaking—as well as the *only* way in which she's consistently orgasmic.

When she's slow to become aroused, 20 percent of the women in our study were best aroused through caressing—ears, lips, buttocks, toes, anything far from her genitals. Kissing is a nice place to start: "I enjoy kissing more than any other foreplay." And stroking the skin, the largest organ of the body, can be especially erotic: "I want hands over my whole body." "Full-body contact arouses me." "Caress *everything.*" Caress "the undersides of my arms," "my shoulder blades, abdomen, top of the mons," "my buttocks, the back of my knees," "inside my thighs, my legs." Kiss, nibble, suck, or massage "my earlobes, the nape of my neck, my eyelids," "my back, belly, and thighs," "the whole of my feet, my toes." For 10 percent of the women, feet and toes were a prominent focus of erotic turn-on.

Women also arouse themselves by stimulating their partners: "The whole physique turns me on, my hands all over his body." "I love to kiss his nipples, explore and tongue his testicles." "His buttocks, chest, and inner thighs, and brushing his cock with my body—textures and touch arouse me."

Caressing a woman's body, far from her genital area, can sometimes trigger orgasm. One woman is orgasmic when her husband simply holds her—"Sometimes after I've come once or twice, we talk and he holds me without other contact, and I come again in his arms"; another, Vivian, when her lover kisses the small of her back or either side of her neck; and another, from kissing one side only—"A neck kiss, only on my right side, can bring my first or a later orgasm. The feeling starts at a spot on the side, and trills down my neck to my pelvis and vagina."

And a few women experience orgasm from general body excitement. Julia is orgasmic when her husband is moaning in bondage; Tracy is often orgasmic in yoga—"It happens when I'm in an inverted position, my head on the floor and my feet in the air, and all my pathways are open—without any other touching, they bubble up out of my body"; and Kristin, the psychotherapist, has been roused to an orgasm in group cele-bration—"Sometimes energy is love and caring, and sometimes it's purely sexual. One summer in California, there were groups of us celebrating—dancing, singing, and just holding hands—and I had an orgasm from just that energy—tightness, heat, and shuddering, every physical reaction."

The body is "all connected." A caring lover lingers, savors his experience, and takes his time to explore a woman's whole sensuous body. He understands how emotions link with physical sensations, and helps her build toward orgasm by making love with adventurous skill, as well as with caring affection.

## Breasts

Most men adore a woman's breasts, and, happily, most women love the sensations arising from having them fondled and kissed: "Tits are sensuous—I need them handled, kissed, and massaged." "Cup the whole breast; for me the outer edges are a place of major turn-on." "I fondle my own breasts at orgasm—and wish that men did more of it."

For many women who are aroused by breast stimulation, the nipple is especially sensitive: "Circling my nipple and areola is the most erotic preliminary." "My hard nipples are fabulously sensitive." "If he gently sucks on my nipples, the feelings travel through my body." Some notes of caution: A few women find their nipples *too* sensitive, particularly during the minutes following orgasm, and prefer that they not be stimulated. Further, some women simply do not enjoy breast or nipple stimulation, or enjoy it "depending on the quality of touch." And finally, some partners overdo a good thing—they continually stimulate the area, rendering it painful or insensitive. Unless partners know otherwise, the best approach is an intermittent touch, with lips, tongue, or fingers nipping, brushing, or gliding in circles, perhaps gently intensified as a woman nears her orgasm.

Of the women in this study, 20 percent have been orgasmic from breast stimulation alone: "Every now and then I can start right off on it, by telling my partner to keep on nibbling, with little bites and caresses, until I come." "Just before I come, my mind concentrates on my vaginal area, even if it started at my nipple." And Michelle: "I like both a soft or aggressive touch, on my nipples or on my full breasts, and sometimes I feel there's a wire from my breasts straight into my vagina. A straight pipeline—all he has to do is touch me there and the feelings go straight down. I have orgasms that way. I'll be still, totally relaxed, concentrating on the feelings, and all of a sudden my whole body shakes involuntarily from head to toe, with rushes, chills, and quivers. . . ."

## Private Places

For a number of women, the labia, both inner and outer, are an area of exquisite sensation. Partners should always include them in clitoral stimulation. Several women are orgasmic from primarily labial touch (with a little clitoral added), and Ingrid —you met her in Chapter 2, speaking of riding right through it together—states that in oral love, she's orgasmic from purely labial sensation.

Ninety percent of the women report being orgasmic from manual-genital stimulation. The ways women prefer it vary greatly. Ginger: "I love it with my clothes on, through underpants or jeans." Coral: "Mainly with my labia, and deep inside my vagina." Other women: "Whole-hand pressure on the area." "All at once—clitoral, vaginal, and anal." "I prefer fingers inside me, very little clitoral." "Vaginal, clit, and my whole pubic mons." "Vaginal, in and out, clitoral, side to side —and please throw in a tongue!" We recall Coral's words— those that started this chapter—that men seem focused on the clitoris. With manual stimulation particularly, many women prefer the vagina, or a combination of vagina and clitoris—or a partner's simultaneous use of mouth, fingers, and limbs . . . all the while caressing her entire responsive body.

Over the course of a lovemaking session, a woman usually fondles her lover's soft or hard penis. Though many women clearly enjoy the texture and throb of a penis, her own excitement mainly stems from her partner's response and enjoyment. Occasionally, she obtains emotional pleasure herself by bringing her partner to orgasm, but usually within a long session, or after she's thoroughly sated her needs and wishes to satisfy his.

Eighty-five percent of the women are orgasmic from cunnilingus, that is, oral stimulation of their genitals, and a few others, though it does not bring them to orgasm, thoroughly enjoy the feelings. For several women a genital kiss gives them their favorite sensations. As one says, "I'm orgasmic from everything, but if I had to give one up, oral or intercourse, at this point I'd stay with oral." For others, oral love is a hallmark of mutuality. Erica, the sculptor: "I don't like to request things, but if a man doesn't make oral love, I'll go down on him. And then, if he doesn't go down on me, I'm a little upset. I might just say something softly, or sort of lie back and expose my body, but I more hope it follows naturally. There are all kinds of gradations, but if it were a constant thing, a constant unwillingness to even try, then I would really be disappointed and feel used. I'd worry that he doesn't really accept and embrace me, and for what reasons? Am I dirty? Is a woman not beautiful? I really like it, and it's an important part of the mutuality."

A woman's complete, abandoned enjoyment of cunnilingus usually takes both time and experience. Ingrid: "I was always orgasmic from manual and oral sex, but I thought oral was very different. For one, I figured if a partner did it to me, I'd have to do it to him, and I didn't want him coming in my mouth. But also, for a while, I just thought it was terrible—that of all the times you shouldn't be orgasmic, it was during oral love. I had a real guilty taboo feeling about that for a long time. I felt I should have warned my partner that I was ready to climax, to let him pull away and have regular sex. But they never seemed to mind—so I never said anything."

And Constance: "At first I wasn't comfortable and would not allow myself to relax, to enjoy the feelings. Then I had a very considerate partner. He let me know he enjoyed it, and that he'd never done oral love with just any passing acquaintance. That's quite flattering to a lady, that a man is that intimate with you and wants you that happy. He would make love to me orally for almost an hour to bring me to orgasm. After that I learned to relax, and it became easier, quicker . . . to *real* easy! Sometimes you just have to kiss my thighs."

And a few women, although they have come to enjoy oral sex, still have substantial reservations. We are reminded of Emily, who always showers when oral sex is probable. These are the feelings of another woman, from a fundamentalist Christian background: "I guess it's because, as a woman, we're so often brought up with the idea that part of us is dirty. For a long time I just couldn't believe that the person stimulating me orally was really enjoying it himself. Once I believed that, it allowed me to enjoy it—but I still have few orgasms orally."

There are other reservations:

My husband likes it more than I do. I prefer him face to face, up here with me.

I can't help it. Even though I love anal intercourse, I still think his mouth on my pussy is dirty.

The stimulation is just too intense, and men don't know how to do it.

After a while, there's not *enough* stimulation, not enough sensation and pressure on my pubic mons, vagina, labia, thighs—all of my body.

We cite these reservations to make several points. Some women simply do not enjoy oral sex, and partners should never pressure them. And many women consider oral sex to be the height of intimacy, more intimate than vaginal intercourse, not to be shared with just anyone. There is also the question of mutuality—if she freely enjoys a man's genital kiss, must she take his penis in her mouth, and moreover swallow his semen?

And finally, the difference between arousing and annoying often borders a hairline. Couples may need to openly converse, and give themselves ample time, before these issues are amicably settled.

All that being said, we hasten to add that for the vast majority of women in this study, oral sex is *marvelously* arousing:

> I *love* it—but men should know it's not only the clitoris, but in and out of my vagina, my labia, thighs, and tummy—anything wet and kissable.

> Wonderful! My vagina and the whole area, and it keeps my clitoris lubricated.

> Fantastic! I wish my partners did it more.

> Wonderful, marvelous. And I love sixty-nine, but it's so exciting, I forget about him and get lost in my own sensations. . . .

As always, body and mind are one, and many women couple sensations with images of themselves. Kate, the woman you met in Chapter 4, who mentally undresses her partners before she decides to go to bed, describes a common experience: "When a man is making oral love to me, sometimes, in my mind, I actually see my clitoris growing. I can feel it getting hard and I think, 'My God, it's just like a man's penis!' I can feel it start to stick out, and when he has his lips on it, I see and feel the hardness."

One last note. When a woman is slow to become aroused, oral sex is mentioned most often as the physical stimulation most likely to get her started.

## The Art of Clitoral Pleasing

Clitoral stimulation, manual or oral, is an art requiring a partner's talent—yet no matter how intuitive or experienced he may be, without a woman's feedback, his success, at best, is erratic. As Tracy stated, the focus of pleasure is a "moving hot spot," differing from moment to moment, and never alike in two women. Of course, many men are insensitive and assume that all women are similar, or simply have no knowledge of how most women function. Dorothy, the peppery redhead you met in Chapter 2, exclaims:

"I can tell you exactly the difference between a good one and a bad one. If a man goes down on you, and the first thing he does is take your clit in his mouth and suck—that's a bad one! If he would just take his tongue and soothe it lightly—that's all he has to do! For some reason they like to suck on it. But it's like a woman giving a blow job—*she* wouldn't just suck, she knows better than doing that. It's different if you're close to an orgasm, then he can use some suction. But before that it's only irritating."

About half the women preferred "indirect" stimulation of the clitoris, and half preferred "direct" stimulation. By "direct," we refer to stimulation of the tip of the glans, where it protrudes from the hood or covering membrane. By "indirect," we refer to stimulation of the sides and top of the hooded clitoris, and of the upper area, toward the pubic mons, where the covering hood, and the clitoris beneath, blend into the body.

Here are some examples of a preference for indirect stimulation, usually involving manual touch:

I like it around the sides of my hood, as well as along my labia. The glans and the top, where the hood blends into my labia, is always much too sensitive.

Light pressure and more spread out, the palm in a circular motion. Most men get too direct and intense.

All over, a broad, circular touch.

I prefer two or three fingers, lightly along the top and sides of the hood. Directly on the tip is much too strong at first, but he can be a bit more direct when I'm excited.

The area at the top of the hood, covering the spot where the clitoris enters the pubis, is often an area of extreme sensitivity. For many women, the area is much too sensitive for comfort; however, for a small number of other women, when they are well advanced toward climax, the area can trigger multiple orgasms.

Here are examples of preferences for a more direct stimulation, usually involving oral sex:

Oral, direct on the glans and under the hood, always works for an orgasm.

Direct, with pressure on the whole area. I love it when he takes his tongue and sweeps from back to front, from my tush through my vagina, across the tip of my glans, and up to the top of my clitoris.

After a while I want it all, direct lapping, off-and-on vibration with his full tongue, and sucking on my clitoris.

Direct and very firm on my glans. It's a little painful at first, but I still like it.

Naturally, a substantial number of women desired both indirect and direct stimulation. A distinct trend emerged—almost every woman who desired both, wished to begin with a light, indirect sensation and touch, then move to more directness, more intensity and mainly *pressure,* only as she neared her orgasm: "An easy, circular pressure and touch—but then at orgasm, steady and direct on my glans, please." "Back and forth, lightly across the hood and even the sides of my legs, then, near orgasm, pressure right on the tip." This is hardly a rule, however—one woman liked the opposite: "I like the feeling in the middle of the hood, left, right, the sides, in a firm, circular motion, but then at orgasm more indirect, spread to the whole vulval area."

Timing and touch is critical. If a lover dwells too long on one spot, or returns too quickly, or applies too much intensity too early, pleasure soon turns to annoyance or discomfort: "I like it strong, and directly under the little hood—but surely not constant, in one place only." "I prefer direct stimulation—but after a big orgasm, please don't touch me for at least five minutes." "Vary the touch and area. Use some movement—and a lot of *imagination.* . . ."

## Arousal by Orally Pleasuring a Man

The great majority of women in this study, some 85 percent, enjoy engaging in oral sex, fellatio, with their lover. Many are highly aroused themselves while orally loving a partner, but a woman's enjoyment is often surrounded by careful qualification. The act is extremely intimate for a woman, and most are highly selective of partners with whom they will try oral love. Enjoying the act for oneself is usually learned over time, and even an adventurous, sensual woman may simply never be charmed: "My husband and I have done—and do—most everything imaginable, and I give him oral sex now and then—but frankly I find it distasteful."

Many women, however, are highly aroused by the act—"I like sixty-nine near orgasm, when his tongue and fingers are in me too, when taking him in oral sex can push me over the edge" —and a handful of women (four, Kristin and Vivian among them) report being orgasmic when fellatio is their only stimulation:

*Wendy:*
I think it's very hot that I can be giving someone
pleasure. I get very turned on, very excited, from going
down on someone, enough to come from that alone,
without other stimulation.

*Tracy:*
It took me a while to like it—and the roof of my
mouth is sensitive. It's orgasmic for me because a lot
of times my emotion is so strong, I so desire the male
body and I know he so desires me, and there's such a
buildup, I get so excited, that when I suck a man,
there must be a release. If it's the first act of love, I
sometimes come without other touching, and I get so
highly aroused that I usually always come when he
comes in my mouth.

This raises a delicate issue: Not every woman appreciates a
partner's ejaculation in her mouth. True, the majority of easily
orgasmic women—a far slimmer majority than those who enjoy
fellatio—sometimes swallow semen, but this is a highly personal act, tightly hedged with caution. Some simply abhor it:
*"Once* was enough!" A few have had disturbing experiences: "I
hated it—men holding my head down." "I enjoy fellatio, but
there was peer pressure to swallow. I did it once but felt forced
—and sick to the pit of my stomach." And others occasionally
accommodate partners, even though they little enjoy doing the
act itself: "I do it when I'm into submission, by telling myself
that I have no choice, but I really feel that I lose femininity—
it's not arousing for me."

For many women, arousal from taking semen in her mouth
only develops with time, or depends on her state of excitement,
or depends above all upon the man and how intimate they have
become: "I wouldn't let my first husband do it—and love it with
my second." "It depends on the person—and how hot I am."

"Men enjoy it, and I especially prefer it on the first day of my period, but a swallow is sometimes the difference between my only liking a man, and liking him a *lot.*"

And, finally, a substantial number of women in this study relish the taking, texture, and taste of a man's ejected semen:

*Bernadette, the ex-nun:*
It excites me to do oral love, and I've grown to enjoy the taste—another hundred calories down!

*Erica:*
I have my lover take some and rub it over my body and breasts. When I masturbate, imagining the taste adds to my excitement.

*Constance:*
It's good protein and surely won't hurt you. I love it because of a man's responses and, if you will, the power I have over him—the fact of taking something soft and bringing him to that point. You can always tell when they're ready by feeling that sensation—they get super hard and vibrate just before they come. You learn to know that point, and I never back off or stop.

Easily orgasmic women integrate physical and mental arousal, and nowhere is this more apparent than when a woman enjoys fellatio. She integrates her tactile sensations with the mental pleasure from her partner's arousal, as well as with the pleasure from her own psychological feelings. Tina is a sales manager in her late thirties, a mother of two children, and a graduate of a boarding school for well-to-do Catholic women. She is tall, lean, and stylish, and speaks with self-assurance: "When I make oral love to a man, I become one with him, I become a part of his penis. We can both be making oral love to each other, and still it's a feeling I get, not a thought, but a feeling of blending. When I get into him, although it heightens my excitement, until after he comes there's no more me and my response but only his sensation. There are times when I'm inside his penis, like seeing inside a little tube, and I can see the come coming. It starts when he's near and then it builds, like there's no more control of my brain and emotions, and he loses control of himself, we both can't hold back any longer, and then it comes to the top in my mind like a creamy, warm little geyser . . ."

Usually a woman who is excited by fellatio enjoys it mainly as a prelude, short of her partner's orgasm—an event she would much rather save for the closer embrace of intercourse. But whether a woman is aroused by fellatio at all, or enjoys a man's semen in her mouth, or enjoys its taste or ingestion—these are extremely personal choices that vary from woman to woman, with partners and situations. All are matters for a *woman* to decide, and for open communication. Common decency dictates that a partner must never force a woman, or even persuade her, to receive in her mouth his uninvited penis or semen. Pressure, persuasion—or surprise—disrupts her arousal, undermines her trust in him, and may destroy her enjoyment of the whole sexual episode.

## Pleasing Yourself

Half the women in this study freely caress their own bodies —skin, breasts, and genitals—while making love, and many experienced partners find it highly arousing. To an adventurous and accepting partner, a woman's self-stimulation might signify that she's "lost control," that she's swept away by passion and overcome by lust.

Yet another half of the women rarely if ever caress themselves while making love with a partner. The reasons are varied. A woman might feel that touching her body is purely her partner's province. And many feel inhibited—"shy" is a common word—and several feel that caressing herself reduces her sensual aura: "Sometimes I'd like to, but I'm embarrassed, and possibly I feel that I'd lose some seductiveness." Other women are mainly concerned with a partner's adverse reaction: "I'm afraid he'd feel threatened, that he'd construe it as meaning he wasn't good enough by himself." "I'd fear he'd think I'm kinky, or more into myself than him." And a woman who never masturbates is unlikely to touch her clitoris, although the very same woman might lovingly touch her breasts.

But a woman is often highly aroused by touching her skin and parts of her body. Particularly when using a rear-entry position for intercourse, or when she needs extra clitoral sensation to be orgasmic during intercourse, and a partner fails or finds it awkward to adequately provide it, a woman might find that self-stimulation gives her total enjoyment:

Sometimes I do it partially, cupping my vulva when his
hands are there, or moving his hand with my fingers,
and I play with my breasts when he does. Men get
very aroused when I'm so excited I need to touch and
masturbate myself.

I love to caress my clitoris when his tongue is in my
vagina or along my lips and inner thighs. When he
takes me from behind, I cup myself with both my
hands for stimulation and pressure.

I'm open about touching myself. Even when I'm riding
on top, I need a lot of moistness and clitoral stroking
and pressure, and I'm never shy about helping my
partner getting me to come—he should enjoy my
pleasure. Most partners like it—I've noticed it gets
some wildly excited—but frankly, if they don't, I just
couldn't care less.

Kate explains her emotions as a feeling of total involvement: "It's exciting to enjoy your own body while each of us is enjoy-

ing the other's body. My legs are so sensitive, my inner thighs
. . . If he's making oral love to me, it's thrilling to know I'm
rubbing my inner thighs or getting my fingers near where his
lips are gliding, and it's very stimulating to him, my being a part
of it. The thought and the feelings, my own sensations, greatly
heighten excitement."

## Anal Petting

The anus is near the genitals, and central to a region of highly
erotic sensation, the buttocks and sensitive skin of the rear inner
thighs. When stimulated, the muscles of the annular ring trans-
mit sensation to adjoining areas. The forward rectal wall borders upon the vagina, and anal muscles contract when a woman
experiences orgasm. The region is convenient and also highly
erotic, and yet it is an area rife with prohibitions, some emotional, some aesthetic, and others based on good hygiene or past
unpleasant experience.

First, let us state a practical caution worthy of repeated
mention. The anus is laden with harmful bacteria. In order to
prevent vaginal infections, a woman (and her *caring* partner)
should never directly proceed from anal stimulation to touching the membranes of the genital area. An exception might arise
when the touch is superficial and the woman has thoroughly
washed, but caution is the best policy. After contact with the
anal region, a partner should wash his hands and, should the
need arise, thoroughly cleanse his penis. And a woman, should
she anally caress a man, should observe caution in touching
herself. Now, if that doesn't turn you off, nothing hereafter is
likely to!

Many adventurous, highly sexed women completely detest
anal touching: "A complete turnoff—yuck!" "I feel it's dirty,
the only thing I won't let my husband do." Coral, a registered
nurse, has never enjoyed the activity "because of aesthetic and
medical issues," and other women fear aggravating recurrent

painful hemorrhoids. And Julia, the woman you've come to know as relishing bondage and swinging, and who is, in pleasurable activities, more than abundantly orgasmic, is thoroughly unnerved by the thought: "If he even mentions anything anal, it disturbs me, and even a finger outside bothers me. It so turns me off that after the subject comes up, it's hard to get even one orgasm with intercourse." Moral: Women must clearly communicate, through words or body language, exactly how they feel about anal stimulation, and partners must be sensitive to a woman's evident wishes. Nothing can more quickly ruin her enjoyment than unwanted anal touching.

That being adamantly stated, let us slowly explore the experience of most of the women in this study. Over two-thirds of the women *sometimes* enjoy anal petting as a part of their lovemaking episode. We emphasize "sometimes," because anal stimulation is a very quixotic pleasure: "Odd, but sometimes it arouses me and sometimes it grosses me out." "Sometimes an anal finger can help bring me to orgasm, yet sometimes it only distracts me." "It depends; sometimes it turns me on and sometimes it doesn't. It's a very sensitive area, and I like it within my control, not someone else's." So a woman's enjoyment of anal stimulation often depends on her partner, her mood, the situation, her state of arousal—and maybe the phase of the moon. Caring partners respect her decisions.

Anal petting encompasses a variety of stimulations, from light external caressing, to slight penetration with finger or tongue, to full, deep finger penetration, and, as noted above, a woman's desires are variable. Whatever the degree of stimulation, the purpose—within this book—is increasing a *woman's* arousal, not indulging a partner. Some men fantasize deep anal penetration of a woman as the acme of his dominance and her absolute loss of control, her willing and eager submission. This is hardly the stuff to help most women reach orgasm.

In any event, a woman who relishes anal stimulation usually

enjoys it in combination with other stimulations, or mainly as a boost across her orgasmic threshold:

> Of course I like an external touch—it's part of making love, and a nice added stimulus. I do it to my husband too.

> No hang-ups here, but a good deep finger can smart for a while before your bottom adjusts to it—and then it's fantastic in combination with deep oral kissing and tonguing.

> A finger inside is a powerful boost to building sexual tension, and I'm particularly orgasmic when it comes near the end of intercourse. I feel so wide and extended that my body just opens and comes.

Turnabout is arousing play. One-third of the women anally pet their partners, varying their technique from a light, external touch to deep, full-finger penetration, and several women say they find it quite exciting to do so: "I love men's asses—and I'm very aroused by petting him." "I love being anally penetrated, and I wanted to do it to him. I assured him he'd get used to it —and you can bet he did." Their petting is often a natural response to their partner's similar caresses: "When we're in sixty-nine, and he pets me with anal sex, my finger goes right up him—I have him where he has me." Some women, having discovered the male prostate, sometimes use it in intercourse as a finishing fillip to orgasm: "Oh yes, a deep finger right near his orgasm sometimes increases his intensity, and prolongs his coming and throbbing." And a few women caution that men also have anal preferences: "He doesn't like it internally." "When I'm really hot, I enjoy anally caressing a man with both my tongue and fingers, but not all men are open to it—better feel him out."

Whether or not to anally pet is purely a woman's decision,

but should she enjoy the sensations, there's no cause to feel guilt. Many easily orgasmic women share her pleasurable experience.

## Anal Intercourse

Remember, the women in this study are hardly "average," and are probably more sexually adventurous than women in the general population.

For many women, the thought of anal intercourse provokes discomfort and loathing. Their feelings are succinctly summarized: *"No way and I never will!"* A number of women tried it once and will not repeat the experience: "I tried once, but it's not for me." "Horrible!—I'll never do it again." Yet over half the women in this study have at least tried anal intercourse, and one-third, on occasion, continue to engage in it.

Frequency and degree of enjoyment vary rather sharply. A few women do it—rarely—simply to please their partners. Others do it infrequently because of their own discomfort: "I enjoy it on occasion, but it's always a bit painful." "I enjoy the sensations, but it messes up my insides for a week. Once a year is fine." Several women have tried and enjoyed it, but have given up the practice for health and medical reasons—including, and growing more prominent, the fear of contracting AIDS. A woman had best be confident of her partner's past sexual conduct. Of further concern, it is possible that anal intercourse, and/or the consequent anal deposit of semen, may impair the body's immune defense against infection. During anal intercourse, a man should use a condom—to protect himself (against urethral infections) as well as his partner.

Grace, who is a registered nurse married to a cardiologist, provides a well-informed comment: "We once enjoyed anal intercourse—in fact I was very orgasmic with it—but my husband and I decided to stop. We were concerned about vaginal infections, and the possibility of an anal fistula and anal muscle damage. But I still enjoy anal sensations, either external or deep, in combination with other stimulations or during vaginal intercourse. Before he inserts a finger, we always make sure I'm well-lubricated, by sliding the vaginal fluids back and soaking the anal entrance."

Grace's comment calls for a note on caring, considerate loving. Before any type of anal penetration, a woman should be substantially aroused and more than abundantly lubricated. Any entry should be made with care. Gentleness, hesitation, a slow, gliding increase of pressure with frequent pauses and even withdrawals can aid her adaptation. An anus is not a vagina, and notions of a thrusting entry should quickly be discarded. It usually is also advisable to keep penetration shallow. In a healthy, natural state the anal muscles are tightly constricted, and the rectum is unaccustomed to sudden, thrusting intrusion. A woman needs time to relax her muscles, and let her mounting erotic feelings overcome those of pain. Yes, pain. Nearly every woman, including those who are orgasmic during anal intercourse, has to get past discomfort or pain before she gets to arousal.

Provided they obtain additional clitoral or other stimulation, 10 percent of the women are orgasmic during anal intercourse. An additional 10 percent report having been orgasmic when full anal intercourse is their only stimulation:

My husband wants it, and sometimes I'll warm up to it. It's a very strong orgasmic combination with clitoral stimulation.

I never think I want it, but I know it's big for men, and sometimes, if I'm greatly aroused, I find myself off and coming. The orgasm is similar to a vaginal, but a really deep and complete one.

I like it for variety, in lots of different positions, like on my back with my legs up high, or on my stomach or doggie fashion. For me the vaginals are stronger, but he more feels the anal contractions.

If a man's penis isn't too big, and I'm feeling "right"— humming hot on a high, high plane—then nothing ever bothers me. I signal I want it by moving my body, and let him take me while I'm passive, anal intercourse, vaginal fingers, clitoris, nipples, breasts . . . the works, any way he wants me.

For Denise, anal sex has become her preference for reaching orgasmic fulfillment. In her mid-thirties, married for sixteen years, she still retains the pert, blond look of an All-American cheerleader. She and her husband enjoyed one foray into open marriage, swinging with another couple—until her oldest child found out, putting an end to the dalliance.

"I come lots of ways—oral, manual, vaginal, anal—but I come from anal intercourse about half the times we make love. Maybe my vaginals are stronger, but anal sex, when he rubs my clitoris, gets me a whole lot quicker.

"I guess I like the feeling of being completely dominated. In vaginal intercourse, I like him on top, or better yet, to take me from behind—but both, I guess, are second to having anal sex. When he's in my vagina and I feel the motion and he penetrates me deeply, the thought of knowing it's in there, my emotions, his physical presence, get me very aroused. I begin to feel on fire from my head to my vagina. I get so heated up that it feels like my temperature is rising, super hot, almost bursting, rising, rising up when I'm at my highest height. Feeling the rising heat gets me into it more because I know there's no stopping me now, I feel that I'm going to come and come and come and burst all over. . . .

"But my favorite come is from anal sex, as well as my favorite fantasy. I've always had this fantasy, before I actually did it, and my husband would like to do it again—he tells me if I find the man, just let him know and he'll be there. I'm in bed with my husband and another man. At first I'm sweet and innocent, and they take advantage of me, take full control, and I've given up my body. They make me do oral sex and touch their physiques all over, then take and caress me and make me screw, and I'm passively kneeling over one who penetrates my vagina, and the other takes me from the rear with deep, complete anal thrusting. . . . In fantasy and real life, by now I've probably come. But I love him to stroke my clitoris, even if it's painful at first, direct and strong all over, and when I'm on my knees like that, my husband behind and reaching around, I often come again. But after the first, the fantasy shifts and now I'm domineering. Even though my husband is taking me as he pleases, in my mind I'm dominant and 'bad,' no longer the sweet little wife, but maybe masturbating one of the men and doing the other oral, or having one still anal, a hand or mouth on the other. The combination of stimulation is absolutely fantastic . . . and I get so carried away that my mind goes completely blank, my stomach knots and the tremors start and all that exists is sensation. . . .

"So maybe he's domineering, but I'm very comfortable with it, I'm being very satisfied with it, a satiating feeling of having sensation both ways. . . ."

For many women, anal intercourse is simply an arousing fantasy, not to be confused—by a man—with her wish to actually do it. Few women completely enjoy penile penetration, and those women who do have usually obtained a very high pitch of prior sexual excitement, if not one or two orgasms.

To be orgasmic, a woman must never accept, and a partner must never press, any sexual activity that undermines her arousal. For most women, anal intercourse meets that description. However, if the thought intrigues you, you might want to try it. For aesthetic and practical reasons, when anal intercourse is possible, many experienced women thoroughly flush the rectum, and a novice should always be sure she uses copious lubrication.

With the precautions previously mentioned, for a few women, occasional anal intercourse adds arousing sensations.

# Becoming Orgasmic During Intercourse 7

> If you want it during intercourse, you've got to have some control—enough to take advantage and go for what hits you off.
>
> —*Tamara*

When we think of sexual relations between a man and woman, our thoughts naturally flow to customary vaginal intercourse. For most of us, intercourse gives a total embrace, and best expresses the sweet combination of intimate love and sex. Intercourse seems the epitome of simultaneous pleasure, of caring mutuality, of overwhelming sensation.

Many women, however, find they are seldom orgasmic during intercourse. A man, provided he gets and maintains an erection, is usually assured of an orgasm through straightforward stroking and friction. Intercourse suits him well. A woman is sexually different, a vastly more complex creature. Her partner might rush her to intercourse, before her extensive erotic system is primed near the threshold of orgasm, and then he might climax rapidly. Or, even should she be highly aroused by lengthy, exciting foreplay, intercourse may serve to reduce, rather than increase excitement. For many women the vaginal canal lacks extreme sensitivity, and a partner's motions may often neglect her needs for clitoral pressure, or pressure upon her vaginal muscles, or even pressure upon a "spot," highly erogenous and personal, somewhere within her vagina. And psychological issues can complicate her orgasm. Perhaps her actions and stimulations fail to match her fantasies, or the extra stimulation she needs is felt to be "wrong" or "unladylike." Or perhaps she is shy about letting her mind develop its own excitations, while her body seeks and fully absorbs divergent but arousing sensations.

The focus of this chapter is how a woman can overcome many of these pitfalls, to become orgasmic during intercourse.

To begin, let us dispose of a misconception. Nowhere is it written in stone that a woman *must* have her orgasms during sexual intercourse. She can have them before or after and still delight in intercourse as a part of her total fulfillment. And, although every woman in this study has been orgasmic during intercourse, some 10 percent always require additional clitoral touching.

Aside from emotional satisfaction, what is a woman looking for in intercourse? First she satisfies physical needs, and then her mental preferences. For half the women, vaginal pressure is paramount, for half, clitoral pressure, and, for the vast majority, both together is heaven. Note the word *pressure*. This description frequently recurs. There are exceptions (and if exceptions suit you, by all means stay with them), but whether vaginal or clitoral, whether obtained through rubbing, thrust, or feelings of stretch and expansion, the ultimate, triggering sensation that a woman desires near orgasm is best described as pressure—broad, sustained, pervasive sensations of clitoral and vaginal pressure.

How does an easily orgasmic woman get her desired sensations? Generally, by knowing her effective positions and, somewhere along the way, making sure she gets them.

Again, as you read these brief descriptions, try to recall the atmospheres surrounding the act of love—the welling of emotions, the sights, sounds, and tastes, fragrances and tactile sensations. Let's listen to some women.

Lily is twenty-five, from a Methodist family background, a beautiful woman whose short brown hair cups the sides of her cheekbones. She has had extensive sexual experience with both men and women: "During intercourse, I have a fantasy in mind, or I visualize my physical sensations, or act upon my feelings, usually those of dominance. Yet I prefer a man on top, to get more vaginal and clitoral pressure, and I move myself up and down, apply myself by lifting my hips and pressing myself against him. But in other situations, when a man doesn't know my responses, it's better to ride on top to control my stimulation."

Another woman: "I like to be on the bottom to control the stimulation. I can direct and move him much better from there —and it's not a question of wanting him to 'dominate.' Even when *he's* on the bottom, a man can move me around, play with my pussy, tits, ass, hips, and be *plenty* dominant."

Natalie: "On top, I can press and control my clitoris. But my best, and we both like it, is probably from the rear—prone, on my knees or side by side with lots of contact and skin. He can play with my clitoris, and I get loads of pressure, by pressing his hand or using my own, and sometimes we talk—I tell him I'm wet and want to be fucked—and all the while my mind is absorbed in abstract, arousing images. . . ."

Iris: "You know I like to be dominant, but I like to screw on my back, particularly with my feet on his shoulders. I get a very deep feeling, can use my vaginal muscles, push him away when I want to, get our hands on my clit, but when I get near orgasm, I want a feeling of fullness, pressure deep up back. I can come on top, but I do it mostly for him, sitting erect and on my knees, like a belly dancer twirling my hips and rippling with my PC's. Doggie style is something else—then I come too quick. It's like he presses a spot, a clit inside my vagina."

Another woman: "I like feeling passive, and what I like most is a guy who can get me off when I'm on the bottom—but I haven't met many men who move themselves right to do it.

Being on top is a more sure thing, so sometimes I start on top, just about get there, quickly switch, and usually it gets me off."

Michelle: "My positions don't matter. I like variety and it depends on my mood. It's fine when my partner's on top—but I know where *I'm* at anyway. I have strong legs, and if it makes him happy to think he's in control, that's swell—but I still know I'm in charge."

Rachel is twenty-one and single, a recent college graduate. Petite and voluptuous, she conveys a delicate quality—along with the no-nonsense air of a woman who likes precision. She describes herself as outspoken and dominant in her daily dealings with people, and yet when she's making love, she always imagines the concept that her lover completely dominates her. Therefore: "I always use my PC's to help me establish a rhythm, and then, near orgasm, I tense and need him deeper in for vaginal pressure and fullness, and hard clitoral rubbing —really a firm, deep pressure on my whole pelvis and pubis. So I don't like my lover to enter from behind because there's not enough stimulation, and I like to see him anyway, to feel he's hovering over me and dominating me physically. I can orgasm from the top—there's enough stimulation—but I don't really like it. In fact, a switch to the top can unarouse me and make me delay a climax, not from physical feelings but because it ruins my thought, the idea of complete submission. So there's nothing as good as the bottom, and I come in two or three minutes."

Ginger: "The only one I don't like is on the bottom. That's because I need a lot of nipple stimulation as a buildup to orgasm, and he can't do it well when I'm under him. The best is on top, sitting tall in the saddle, my legs bent and feet tucked under him. I sink myself into hitting my cervix, sort of a bouncing, trampoline effect, but at orgasm I hold the tip of his penis hard and firm against it, and when the nipples start to hurt, I know I'll go right to orgasm, and I roll my pelvis forward and spread the lips of my vulva so hairs will brush my clitoris, and then I push against him until it pulses and quivers. The rear is pretty good too—from there I can sometimes have doubles, one when he gets my nipples and clit, and another with anal, a finger, as well as, of course, my nipples."

Well, you get the drift—every woman is different. But let's introduce some order, and make a few suggestions on how to assist your arousal.

### • *Control Your Sensations*

This is the most consistent theme that runs through the varied descriptions. A woman might play for hours, and let her lover enjoy himself in ways that amuse and arouse him, but when she desires an orgasm, she usually assumes a position to control her own sensations.

Until you're orgasmically fluent, lay aside any notions of simultaneous climax. Few women mentioned it as a goal they ever strive for. Approaching orgasm, keep your mind on yourself; after you've been satisfied, there's time to delight your partner. Anyway, assuming they're not kept a secret, your own orgasmic responses will often trigger his.

A woman usually has greater control when she rides a man on top. On top, she can better control penetration (and some women do *not* enjoy extremely deep penetration), and then, approaching orgasm, better sustain or increase sensation. She can vary clitoral contact and then maintain better pressure. If she needs a final boosting tension just prior to orgasm, she can flatten herself and tighten her legs, rubbing hard against him. However, don't forget the women who feel they have greater control from the bottom. From the bottom—unless a partner resists her efforts—some women feel greater "leverage," greater tension and pressure, yet can still control and pace their lovers by using their arms and legs, vaginal muscles and pelvis. Entry from the rear affords the least control; in most cases, for a woman to be orgasmic when entered from behind, a partner should know her needs, or a woman should clearly show him.

• *Position Yourself for Specific Sensations*

Explore your body in intercourse. Get to know your every response and every exquisite sensation in every inviting position. When you find the most arousing ones, go to them near orgasm, and ride them into elation.

Until you're orgasmically fluent, lay aside any notions of exotic, gymnastic positions. Most are ineffective for getting essential sensations, and no woman mentioned one as affording consistent orgasms. Save them for a playful mood or experimental sessions.

Approaching orgasm, many women desire the feeling of deep vaginal pressure. For some this feeling is best obtained when making love on the bottom. She can spread or lift her knees; lift her pelvis; place her legs on his shoulders; wrap her legs around his back and press him in with her heels. As a plus, all these movements usually obtain additional clitoral contact. Approaching orgasm, she can straighten her legs to increase her tension, and rub her partner against her vulva or press herself against him; spread her legs and pull him in, also enjoying the pressuring weight against her thighs and buttocks; slide herself down or slide him up in a "riding high" position, increasing the rubbing pressure against her PC's and clitoris.

Other women prefer these sensations when riding on top of a lover. Approaching orgasm, she can get deep vaginal pressure by sinking down and holding, or go for a plunging effect, varying pressures and angles. Others go for a different sensation, elsewhere within the vagina; on top she can freely move side to side, forward and back or in circles. When she knows she wants clitoral pressure, the top affords more certainty. She can flatten herself and tighten, or roll her clitoris into him.

From the rear, she can also get deep, deep pressure, particularly when on her knees, with her head inclined to the bed. Or, with her partner's penis angled up, she sometimes wants rectal pressure, or pressure on the forward wall, his penis angled downward.

In any event, an easily orgasmic woman is extremely aware of specific sensations that usually bring her to orgasm. When she gets down to pleasurable business, when she feels that her moment approaches, chances are she's positioned herself to reach a peak of enjoyment.

### • Position Yourself for Added Sensations

Many women choose a position because it affords a chance for the added stimulations which they find sublime or essential. When, to be orgasmic during intercourse, a woman needs additional clitoral stimulation, she certainly makes sure she's positioned to get it. The bottom presents some difficulties. When stretched full-length on a woman, it's hard for a partner to use his hand to touch her clitoral area without interrupting lovemaking. Her partner might kneel upright, keeping full penetration while massaging her breasts and clitoris, but full-body contact is lost. She can also bend or raise her legs, and use her own hand or hands. However, women who like manual-clitoral touching during intercourse often find that their preferred positions are side by side, woman-on-top, or entry from the rear. And a combination of rear and side with her leg thrown over his often affords the best combination of sensual touching and thrust. The man or woman can touch alone, or either can place their hand on the other's or keep their fingers entwined— helping to guide and instruct concerning location, intensity, pace.

But there are other sensations. Ginger, for example, likes positions that enable nipple and breast stimulation. Other women want closeness, the feel of full-body contact, or a position that allows them to view themselves or their partners. They also might want an anal touch, or a caressing of their buttocks, abdomen, or inner thighs, or to be able to keep on kissing throughout the length of intercourse.

• *Position Yourself for Emotional Pleasure*

A position that enhances your mood is likely to increase arousal. Be sure to use it at least for a while during sexual intercourse, and, if it also provides good physical stimulation, make sure you're there near orgasm.

For some women, like Rachel, the psychological component is often decisive for orgasm. If it's arousing to feel submissive, be sure you're positioned to believe it. Other women enact a role in which they're aggressive or dominant, and usually the top position enhances their total excitement. Fantasies, roles, and moods tend to suggest positions.

All these factors—controlling sensations, obtaining specific sensations, adding sensations, and using emotional preferences —are best used in combination. Imagine what you can do, the infinite possibilities. However, until you're orgasmically fluent (or have found a definite orgasm-triggering, pleasurable vaginal area), never neglect your clitoris. Whether on top, bottom, or side, begin with "coital alignment" techniques—keeping yourself in position for constant clitoral contact.

As developed in the following chapter, three-quarters of the women described one or more areas of special vaginal sensitivity. However, an equal number of women were aware that their orgasms during intercourse usually or always depended upon some—or a large—degree of continuing clitoral stimulation. For the great majority of women, orgasm-triggering vaginal sensations do not exist by themselves, but are intertwined with clitoral sensations. And many of the women who report being orgasmic from "exclusively" vaginal stimulation desire extensive clitoral stimulation "as a starter," or state that a prior clitoral orgasm "makes it easier" to obtain an orgasm through vaginal stimulation. In nearly all cases, clitoral sensations help to "prime" a woman, creating arousal and vasocongestion throughout her genital system. And, of course, a substantial minority of women find that purely clitoral sensations—together with breast and nipple, and other full-body sensations—are their *sole* physical source of every experienced orgasm.

As Coral said in the previous chapter, there's a lot of territory out here. . . .

Tamara is thirty and married, from a Jewish family background. She is shy, pixieish, supple, an aerobics dance instructor who has recently gained her masters degree in sport physiology.

"I love a long foreplay. We talk and play and tell each other what we would like and what feels good. He kisses and touches my nipples and breasts, then around my labia and clitoris, and then when I'm wet and excited, his fingers go up my vagina. When I'm feeling really hot, I get on top and flatten myself, or sometimes lean back so his hands can caress the sensitive parts of my body.

"I tease myself with his penis. The tip is real important to me, the feelings I get from teasing myself, exciting my clitoris and labia, and I see his penis and tip in my mind exactly as you would draw it, thicker and longer than average. With his big tip there's a lot of sensation, and when I'm on top I play with his penis, soaking up feelings and seeing the tip, tantalizing and shallow—and all of a sudden it's in me, and I feel a rippling, shocking feel when the whole penis plunges deeper, stretching out my vagina. After a while I'll tighten up and get the feel of a rhythm, gripping him with my vaginal muscles, seeing and feeling his penis move, his tip up toward my cervix.

"Then I'll bear down, pressing his tip in deeper, coming closer and closer, setting a slow, hard rhythm, and pressing against his pubic bone, his penis moving in and out, catching the tip of my clitoris—and then when he touches my breasts, my mental focus suddenly shifts because that connection's happening. Stimulation hits, and I feel excitement go from my breast all the way to my clitoris, and I picture a network firing, all these little axons shooting exciting pulses, zipping down my body from the breast he's kissing or touching. Or maybe like little capillaries, fibers in my breasts directing on one narrow artery, coursing down my body, then branching around my clitoris and deep inside my vagina. The pictures shoot back and forth, but just before I'm coming my mind is all on the penis mixed with my own sensations.

"I'm moving slower and harder, tensing everything, squeezing out . . . then holding him deep and tight for an instant, gripping him up inside, holding tight with my arms, pressure on my clitoris, pressure deep inside me—and then the explosion hits . . . hard, explosive contractions start inside my vagina and vulva and radiate through my body, exploding from inside to out. . . ."

. . . and it's all connected.

## Intercourse and Satisfaction

Can a woman feel satisfied without sexual intercourse? Yes, assuming she was orgasmic from other stimulations, one-third of the women felt satisfied even though vaginal intercourse was not a part of a particular lovemaking encounter. Their reasoning varied from the physiological ("If I come ten times from oral sex, I don't need intercourse") to the practical ("If his penis is too large, I'll prefer him to come with oral sex and have him return the favor") to the interpersonal ("It's easier to arouse me with oral sex anyway, and there's no need to put performance pressures on my lover") to the emotional ("I can still feel loved without intercourse"). Without intercourse, most women found satisfaction through orgasms from oral sex.

A few women wanted "both," an orgasm from foreplay as

well as from sexual intercourse. This desire might be felt as necessary ("I need an orgasm from foreplay, either manual or oral, before I'm orgasmic in intercourse") or as a requirement for total satisfaction ("The sensations are just different, an orgasm from oral and intercourse, and I usually want both for complete satisfaction").

Two-thirds of the women usually or always desired intercourse. Now and then their needs were physiological. A woman may be orgasmic only during intercourse, or she may need vaginal feelings to experience complete physical release: "I need it and want it for my deepest orgasms—but I'd never lay that on a partner." But, whether or not she's orgasmic during intercourse, most women wanted it for complete *emotional* pleasure:

It's not even close! I need that penetration and the feeling of being filled. I guess, subconsciously, I think that's how it "should" be.

I may be more aroused with oral—or whatever—but intercourse is the *real thing.*

Intercourse is God's great gift of oneness. I want to be close, to be filled, I want to have an orgasm, and I want my man to come in me.

I can play with myself and have an orgasm. With a partner I enjoy the closeness of intercourse; it's the true essence of sexuality and—this may sound ridiculous—I figure as long as I'm doing it, I might as well have orgasms.

I like the feeling of having him inside me. It doesn't feel right, like something is missing, if we don't finish making love with intercourse.

We might note that many women who have had their fill of orgasms, and who realize they're unlikely to have another, still desire intercourse to have a sense of closeness and completion.

## Surefire Arousal

Every man has faced this circumstance: He's making love to a woman and she's simply not getting aroused—what does he do next? For that matter, what does a *woman* do next? We asked this question: "If you are having difficulty becoming aroused, is there any 'most often surefire' stimulation you seek that usually is able to turn you on?"

Intercourse may be satisfying to round out or finish a sexual encounter, but if a woman is slow to respond, it is also the least propitious way to begin her sexual arousal. Of all the women in this study, *not one* suggested intercourse as the way to stir her excitement and begin her buildup to orgasm. If she is already in intercourse, she tries to change positions or tactfully interrupt intercourse and start arousal again.

To initiate arousal, a slight majority of women mentioned a form of genital stimulation. Oral sex was most often favored, followed by manual-clitoral touching, then intravaginal and labial caresses. A few women mentioned anal caresses, or helping her partner stimulate her, or fondling her partner's genitals, or performing mutual oral sex, or taking him with fellatio. At least one-third of the women talked of non-genital touching. A body caress was most favored—kissing, nibbling, touching, massaging or stroking the feet, legs, and thighs; the buttocks, abdomen, nipples, and breasts; the back, shoulders, neck, or eyes. Of non-genital areas, nipple stimulation, often through sucking or tonguing, most often incited arousal.

For a substantial minority of women, initiating arousal is primarily a matter of mental or emotional stimulation. A woman needs "sweet, caring talk" with her partner, or "dirty, dominating talk," or "romantic talk." She needs to "feel affection," to be "stroked and hugged," to feel she is "being taken with passion." Or "a favorite fantasy" helps, or "imagining pretty places and people," or getting into a mood by "implying submission" or "acting dominant." Sometimes "knowing a lover's aroused" becomes the key to excitement.

A handful of women resort to "externals," such as erotic movies and books, a vibrator, or drugs. And another small group of women simply refuse to be bothered: "If I'm not aroused, I'll get irritated if I'm pressed." *"Forget it.* If I have to try, I don't want to be aroused."

And, of course, many women need combinations—erotic words and oral sex, or fantasy and sucking her nipples, or oral and manual genital sex while a lover massages her thighs and nape and tells her how much he loves her.

Several themes stand out. If a woman is slow to become aroused and she wishes to be orgasmic—by any means as well as during intercourse—she usually should resist (and a partner should never press) a headlong rush to intercourse.

Second, most orgasmic women have, as Tracy phrased it in Chapter 1, "a little ace in the hole" to get her excitement started. When the ace is within her control, or can be communicated to her partner, a woman should freely play her cards to build her sexual arousal.

The final persistent theme revolves around emotions. Coupled with genital kissing and touch, breast and body caresses, the most surefire sexual excitement springs from affection and caring.

## Totality of Sensation

For orgasmic women, making love is a joyous adventure that builds her sensations toward orgasm. Here we have focused on physical sensations, but that is only half the story. Future chapters explore the ways in which orgasmic women compound and weave excitement from erotic mental activity.

To be orgasmic, many women desire or need a great totality of sensation. Sensation compounds and accumulates, and orgasmic women create and build enough to cross the threshold. When asked which physical stimulations were most effective for orgasm, a majority of women responded by citing a sequence or combination. For example: "First kissing, then manual, then an oral orgasm, followed by deep vaginal intercourse with his hands all over my body, gives me my most intense orgasm." "Taking turns caressing each other, then doing sixty-nine, then oral and anal on me, then my best positions to get vaginal and clitoral together—a whole sum of sensations." "All simultaneously—oral, manual, breast, and anal." "Intercourse while kissing, fondling my thighs and breasts, and working my vaginal muscles." "Oral with his hands on my nipples." "Intercourse with anal—plus kissing my nipples and breasts—while getting clitoral pressure."

But don't get stuck in a rut, for these are never "formulas." Needs and moods constantly change, often from moment to moment, and making love is an art, an interplay of freedom and creative sensitivity.

Approaching orgasm, a woman tends to concentrate on one outstanding sensation, though some enjoy a final boost, an added strong sensation that overfills her cup and carries her into orgasm. Along the way, however, most every woman expressed her knowledge that she builds and creates arousal through totality of sensation—a total exquisite sum of erotic physical pleasure.

# Physical Variety

It's amazing—I have so many multiple orgasms, and
fluid just squirts out of me sometimes, like when a man
ejaculates. But it's also disturbing. . . . I've wondered if
I'm normal.

—*Peg*

At one time or other, every woman wonders if, physically,
she's sexually "adequate" or sexually "normal." Her concerns may be influenced by popular myths, or by the exploits
and fantasies of women friends and male partners, or by current
knowledge and theory about sexuality—whether she has this or
that erogenous area, whether she makes love or responds in a
certain way, or whether her physical peculiarities and preferences match up with prevailing "standards."

Yet every woman is an individual—psychologically, of
course, but also physiologically. This chapter will explore some
current issues in sexology, and through these issues underscore
the wondrous multiplicity of what is sexually normal. By the
end of it, whatever your physical endowments or preferences,
it is likely you will find that you fall within the broad range of
normal—and that you need not have fabulous "equipment" to
become more easily orgasmic.

## The G Spot . . . Plus X, Y, and Z Spots

Do women have areas of vaginal sensitivity that, without
clitoral stimulation, can trigger the orgasmic response?

We would probably not bother to ask this question had Freud

not implied that "mature" female orgasms arose from vaginal stimulation alone. To correct Freud, and square scientific interpretation with the experience of the great majority of women, Kinsey, then Masters and Johnson, emphasized the continuing —if not exclusive—role of clitoral stimulation in building sexual arousal and triggering the female orgasmic response. Thus, many women who subjectively knew that some of their orgasms were indeed triggered by vaginal stimulation worried about their normality. Then, after *The G Spot* was published in 1982, the pendulum began to swing back toward an emphasis on "vaginal" orgasm. Many women went searching for a new magic spot, only to find they did not possess such a "sexually functional" area—one that produced pleasurable and effective sexual response.

The G spot was named after Ernst Grafenberg, who described the general area, and its potential sexual functions, in scientific journals in 1944 and 1950. It has been described as a bean-shaped area, about the size of a dime or quarter, which lies within the anterior wall of the vagina (the front wall, toward the mons and navel), usually about halfway between the pubic bone and the cervix. Underlying this area, and deeper within or along the front vaginal wall, is the urethra and neck of the bladder. A network of glands and ducts, considered to be a vestigial or nonfunctional counterpart of the male prostate, surrounds the urethra and also underlies the lower half of the front wall of the vagina. Some researchers have suggested that when the G-spot region is stimulated with a deep, firm pressure, it may swell and even trigger orgasm. However, other researchers have questioned the existence of *any* vaginal area capable of triggering orgasm without continuing clitoral stimulation, while still others have suggested that *many* areas within the vagina are capable of triggering orgasm.

Based upon our conversations with easily orgasmic women, we harbor little doubt that *some* women do have a region of vaginal sensitivity that approximates the G spot. Without using the term "G spot," we asked the women whether they had any vaginal areas that were "particularly sensitive," or that gave rise to "particularly pleasurable feelings," or that they "preferred stimulating." Fifteen percent of the women provided accurate descriptions of an orgasmic response resulting from stimulation of an area which corresponded to the G spot, and another 15 percent gave "quite possible" descriptions of the area, although stimulation of it did not necessarily produce an orgasm.

Paula had never heard of the G spot. She is an artist in her mid-thirties, a large-framed woman from a Jewish background: "Oh yes, yes, I have a great place in there. It's up around the corner somewhere . . . up behind the pubic bone and toward the front. When I'm hot and he hits it, I have premature orgasms —I mean just a couple of touches and it goes. Sometimes I have them when he rubs it hard with his fingers, and sometimes with his penis. I can get his tip at that area when I'm on top, leaning far back or far forward, but the very best way to get it is doggie style from the rear—at orgasm I flatten out and let him slide much deeper, pressing past that part as I come."

A few women, such as Vivian, said they had experienced G-spot orgasms before they had read of the area's existence: "I've had that for a long time—I knew it, but I couldn't explain it. A lover I had was completely convinced that a clitoral climax is all there is to it, but I told him, 'No, it isn't all there is, because if you don't enter me, I can have a dozen orgasms and I still ache inside and it's not enough. I still have to be penetrated. The feeling inside just doesn't go away with only a clitoral orgasm.' The area is probably a couple inches inside my vagina, toward the upper or front part. I don't have to be penetrated very deep to get that sensation, for that ache to go away. His fingers can reach it, and John, my lover now, does that sometimes when he's already worn out, because I always tell him when I need more. With his penis, the most satisfying way is when I'm on top, because then I can push right against him and rub it the way I want to. And we do that almost every time, toward the end of our session, because, although I can build it up and come several times that way, the last one is usually my final, satisfying orgasm."

There is increasing evidence that vaginal sensitivity is not confined to one small "spot" in the vagina, but, in many women, may encompass whole "areas" which extend along the anterior or frontal length of the vagina, or along the lower half of the rear vaginal wall. Several women describe what may be termed a "continuity" of sensation: "In the G literature they talk about the feelings from a G orgasm as being so different, but I haven't found it to be that way. Sometimes I put a pillow under my hips and begin an orgasm from shallow 'G' thrusting, but then I have a tendency to arch my back, to pull him into me for a deeper thrust, and my most intense feelings are from a very deep vaginal area where I guess I have more uterine contraction. But the two areas and sensations seem interrelated, a straight flow one to another."

A few women, such as Michelle, describe distinct vaginal areas, each capable of producing orgasm: "I've thought about this a lot, and I'm sure I have two different spots! I recently read about a spot—I guess it's called the G spot—and I experience that lower in my vagina. I can only find that with penetration from the rear or with his hand. But there's another spot, an extremely high or deep one. I can get that one in all positions —if I can find it—and it feels like a pressure or touching way up inside my stomach. I try to look for it and to remember the feelings and sensations when I've found it, but it's not always there, or it's there and it's gone, or it just gets to feeling so good that I forget to remember anything!"

And many women describe particular sensitivity in the vaginal areas that overlie their flexing PC muscles. Other women are sensitive in the regions bordering their labia, often corresponding to the "orgasmic platform" area, where vasocongestion builds prior to discharge at orgasm.

In all, three-quarters of the women described one or more

areas of special vaginal sensitivity. However, as mentioned in the previous chapter, to be orgasmic during intercourse, most also needed continuing clitoral stimulation as well.

Generally, these sexually adventurous women have been uninhibited in exploring their bodies and sexual capabilities, yet only a small minority have found vaginal regions capable of triggering orgasm without other simulation. No woman should be disappointed if she doesn't find such an area. Moreover, a few women have explored for a G spot only to find that pressure or rubbing in the area causes discomfort, or a need to urinate even though the bladder is empty. These sensations are hardly the kind to foster arousal and orgasm. A woman must always respect herself and her own pleasures and preferences.

## Female "Ejaculation"

Is a woman capable of ejaculating? And if so, is she "normal"? No other sexual response can cause more astonishment —as well as consternation: "The first time it happened, I thought I wet the bed!"

Ejaculation must be distinguished from normal vaginal lubrication. Vaginal lubrication is a woman's initial physical sign of mounting sexual arousal, analogous to the stirrings of a man's erecting penis. When she becomes excited, when her body *knows* she's become excited, her clitoris starts to swell and her genital region congests. Droplets of moisture seep through her vaginal walls, eventually coating her vaginal folds with slippery, glistening fluid. The amount of lubrication may ebb and flow during lovemaking, but her juices and moist sensations tell her she's aroused.

It is easy to confuse extra-copious vaginal lubrication with episodes of ejaculation. Nevertheless, we asked the women whether they ever experienced episodes when a "greater than average" amount of fluid was expelled during sexual contact.

We have mentioned a network of ducts and glands, extensively developed in some women, which underlies the G-spot region, perhaps extending to the neck of the bladder. It is possible that these structures accumulate a "fluid" which, in a few women, is slowly released or forcibly expelled through the urethra during sexual activity. Five percent of the women provided descriptions of ejaculatory episodes that are clearly different from copious lubrication, and another 10 percent described occasional possible occurrences.

Peg, twenty-one, is a high-school graduate who was raised by adoptive parents in Virginia. When she married, she and her husband settled in Ohio, where she recently gave birth to her first child. She declares herself to be "dominant" in interpersonal relationships, yet somehow projects a sweet, wistful, and hesitant quality. Peg is ultra-orgasmic, capable of twenty to thirty orgasms in an average lovemaking session. She describes her clitoris as "very large and sensitive, sticking out at least a half inch whenever I get excited.

"I usually need clitoral contact for my first orgasm. Either I'm touching it or he is, or it's rubbing on his pubic bone or something. After the first, my vagina and my clitoris and everything's more sensitive, and it's easier to orgasm again. At least once every time we have intercourse, at some orgasm, my muscles all contract and contract and contract and this fluid pushes out like a man's ejaculation. I don't know where it comes from and I don't know why it happens, but it always happens at least once, and sometimes more than once, at the beginning, middle, or end of a session. It usually happens during intercourse, penetration, but after it's happened once with his penis, it can happen again with his fingers inside me. It's just . . . incredible. It explodes. I've sprayed five feet and soaked my husband's feet. We need to have a mattress cover, and we keep lots of towels around the bed. After we make love, we change the sheets and shower."

Rather than a G-spot region in the anterior wall of her vagina, Peg describes a sensitive area in the posterior wall, toward her spine and rectum: "I like the pressure and rubbing to be back and down toward the rear. When I'm on top, I tilt forward and rub my clit, and his penis presses the back of my vagina. If he comes and I haven't had enough yet, I lie on my back and he continues to stimulate me with his fingers—up to four with his palm facing down—pressing and rubbing the bottom and rear, sometimes pretty far up me."

Most women note that it is quite difficult to distinguish specific vaginal areas during the throes of lovemaking. When Peg expels fluid, it is quite possible that the shaft of her husband's penis, or the back of his fingers and hand, is also massaging an anterior area of the vagina near the ducts and glands surounding her urethra. Nevertheless, we must never ignore a woman's subjective and individual experience; for Peg, her sensitive vaginal region lies along the posterior wall of her vagina.

Julia describes an experience that is somewhat similar to Peg's: "Sometimes it's almost like I've urinated. That strong, I go off and just shoot it . . . a flood. And that happens very often, at least once, sometimes in the beginning or middle—every time is different. Sometimes it finishes me off completely, but usually it just gets me started—and I'm like dynamite if you touch me after. Any stimulation can do it, intercourse, oral, or manual."

And Michelle describes two differing experiences, one a strong expulsion, the other a slow release: "The first time, I was *sure* I'd wet the bed—in fact it felt very similar to when my water broke when I was delivering my first baby. I do have the fluid more often when he enters from behind—usually when he penetrates, but sometimes at my orgasm—and then it is usually a gush. But I've had another experience. Sometimes, if I'm really keyed up emotionally, it's like a continual small amount, pulsating, regular, like you were squeezing an eyedropper. You know, just bomb, bomb, bomb . . ."

There is little doubt that some women expel a fluid, other than vaginal lubricant, during sexual activity. At present, it is not known whether the fluid comes directly from the bladder, or whether it emanates from the ducts and glands surrounding the bladder neck and urethra, or from both—or from elsewhere. Further, the chemical composition of the fluid is still undergoing research—whether it resembles urine (or *is* urine), or whether it resembles a man's prostatic fluid. In any event, the women who expel such fluid voice a subjective opinion that it is "not urine." They usually describe the fluid as "clear and whitish," without the characteristic odor of urine. The frequency and amount of fluid can vary widely, from "at least once each lovemaking session" to "once in a blue moon," and from "a tablespoon" to "a flood." The triggering stimulation need not be G-spot stimulation, or occur during intercourse, or even be entirely vaginal—cunnilingus, perhaps with some intrusion of the tongue within the tumescent vagina, can sometimes trigger a discharge.

Expelling large amounts of such fluid can cause a woman great concern. If an expulsion of fluid is accompanied by pain, or if she has a history of urinary incontinence, or if there is the slightest possibility of a urinary or other infection, a woman should consult her doctor.* However, barring these circumstances, she may be confident that she shares this characteristic with many other women.

Naturally, a woman need not "ejaculate" to be easily orgasmic. The vast majority of women in this study have never had this experience.

## More Alphabet: PC Muscles

Can a woman increase her orgasmic capacity through active use of her PC muscles?

---

*For that matter, any woman who truly desires orgasms and has difficulty obtaining them after an extended period of trying should consult a qualified physician (she may have a physiological dysfunction) and/or a qualified therapist.

The pubococcygeal, or PC, muscles are a bowl-shaped sheet of muscles, also known as the circumvaginal musculature, which surround the middle third of the vagina and, at orgasm, suddenly convulse with rhythmic, involuntary contractions. It is also possible for a woman to voluntarily contract these muscles, creating pelvic sensation through flexing within the muscle itself. During intercourse, she can squeeze them around the penis—which also can give her partner a range of exquisite sensations.

Many ancient cultures encouraged a woman to train and use her circumvaginal muscles—after all, Cleopatra had a *lot* going for her. In 1952, Arnold Kegel sparked contemporary interest in this muscle group by suggesting that active toning and use of the muscles—originally prescribed as a cure for urinary stress incontinence—could have substantial benefits for a woman's sexual satisfaction. In time, after self-administered toning exercises commonly known as "Kegels," some requiring simple, repeated voluntary flexing, others requiring "resistance training" (flexing against an inserted object such as her fingers, or a device designed to measure pelvic muscle strength), a woman can increase the thickness and strength of her circumvaginal muscles. More information will be found in the books cited in our bibliography, but here are some practical hints for finding your own PC's:

Since your PC muscles also control the flow of urine, you can identify them by stopping the flow of urine midstream. Try it, stopping the flow off and on if you can, but always be sure to empty your bladder after your explorations. Do not be discouraged if it's difficult at first—we're sure Cleopatra practiced. Be sure your legs are spread; this helps you isolate your PC sensations from those of your anal and buttock muscles. And then remember the feelings—in time they will be your friends.

The great majority of women in our study consciously and actively use their PC muscles during a lovemaking session. Many use them in an intermittent and random fashion, or primarily for the pleasure of their partners: "My muscles are in good shape, but I don't consciously think of them. When I do, it blows his head off." "We both get some pleasure, but it's more to play with him and arouse him, or as he's approaching orgasm, but it's nothing regular. Anyway, I seem to lose control when I get near orgasm myself." For a majority, however, flexing the PC muscles greatly increases their personal sensations as well as those of their lovers. And a substantial minority of women often or always use their PC's to add enough additional sensation to bring them to the threshold of orgasm—and sometimes to boost them over.

Women vary greatly in their preferred patterns and timing of use:

*Rachel, the twenty-one-year-old who prefers the bottom position to further her concept of being dominated:*
It's just something I do, but not "consciously." I use it at the beginning of penetration, maybe for thirty seconds or a minute, sometimes to arouse my partner but mainly to induce a rhythm, a thrusting pattern. Later on I can hold off orgasm by changing the rhythm, or I can hasten it if I constrict quickly.

*Lisa:*
I use them for myself, both in oral and intercourse. It feels better when I can establish my own regular rhythm.

*Kate:*
I love to tease a man, of course—tightening usually arouses him. But if I'm having trouble with a vaginal orgasm, and I can't feel the man, then squeezing helps my sensation. Sometimes, by using my PC's, I can come without much clitoral stimulation.

*Mimi, who requires continuing clitoral stimulation to reach orgasm:*

I discovered I could use my PC's through breathing exercises for singing. In intercourse, and masturbation, somewhere around the middle, I begin to tighten and release until I'm close to orgasm—then I tense and hold it tight right on through the climax.

A few women actively work their PC's until they near an orgasm, when further conscious use disrupts their concentration or their feelings of "letting go" and surrendering to sensation. However, other women *initiate* use as orgasm approaches:

*Kristin:*
I use it a lot. After I had my children, I used to exercise regularly to tighten up my insides. Now, near orgasm, it happens automatically—regular squeezes, then a steady hold into orgasm. Three or five seconds of steady tension helps assure my climax.

*Ginger:*
I Kegel every day, while driving my car, or whenever I'm by myself, or even during conversations—like here during this interview. I learned it in six steps, in Lamaze classes, so that's how I do it in intercourse. It helps me mentally focus on the area and magnifies the intensity. Six increasing steps going up—tingle, tighten, relax; tingle, tighten, relax . . . The last Kegel is a final push that takes me into orgasm.

*Ingrid:*
I was orgasmic before I ever used my PC's but I get more intense, longer-lasting orgasms doing it, with both intercourse and manual. Close to orgasm, I give it two or three tightenings, and then hold—and keep it held— to give myself stronger sensation.

Well-toned circumvaginal muscles also increase the strength of the involuntary contractions of orgasm. Peg, for example, the multiorgasmic woman who always expels some fluid, reports: "After a few months of intercourse, I began to feel loosened inside. Without having read about it, I just began to exercise and flex the muscles deep inside to help me feel tight. Now, at orgasm, usually without my thinking about it, my PC's sometimes tense to the actual expulsion of my husband's penis. Both of us can feel it; contractions seem to start at the top and then work down my vagina."

Some women use their PC muscles to help bring on additional orgasms. Grace relates her experience: "My first orgasm is so natural that I don't really work at it, but during that in-between time I use my PC's to help bring myself to another orgasm. You feel the man much more, and I find that brings a very heavy and sometimes simultaneous climax. There's a nice effect going on because you're concentrating on the muscles, feeling sensation along with images of colors, and it's almost like actually feeling the penis going against the wall. I mean it's a very sensual . . . very gliding sensation."

A few women, after prolonged and dedicated training, are able to exert a delicate and selective control of their circumvaginal muscles. Amy is in her mid-thirties, a solidly built, softspoken woman with swirling long auburn hair. Now divorced, she was rarely orgasmic during ten years of marriage, a problem she attributes to her husband's "lack of staying-power" and her own low self-esteem: "About five years ago, I decided it was good to have orgasms, and I decided to learn how to do it for myself regardless of how long my partner lasted. I read about using my PC muscles, where it's like you're urinating and you hold back, and I could feel where the muscles were and I realized I could do it. I just thought about it, just kept working on it, and I've trained myself to do it at any time. I use my PC's during oral sex and, in fact, even when I'm alone in bed—if I work my PC's, and visualize my muscles moving and picture in my mind my clitoris responding, I can have an orgasm without touching myself.

"In intercourse, I can move one muscle versus another, one vaginal wall versus the other side. As I'm doing it, in my mind I think of it more as side to side, whatever side I want to move down and contract, rather than back and forth or in and out. Like a suction, making a suction or pumping motion, up and down. During penetration, depending on the thrust he's using, I can tighten it and loosen it, or leave it completely tight a long time, or completely loosen the muscle and just let it go. I can go, say, from left to right, and then stop and reverse it, move right to left, or move all the way around him, caressing his penis in circles. It's voluntary, but I don't work against him—it's the way I'm reacting to what's going on. Most men are shocked I can do it. When I feel he's close to coming, a few quick squeezes bring me up to an orgasm right away."

A few women offered some reservations on using their circumvaginal muscles. For one woman, Julia, any use was distracting and caused her to lose concentration. For some women, using the PC's can sometimes result in an involuntarily delayed climax. Occasionally a woman can squeeze too hard or maintain pressure too long, causing her lover discomfort, or bruising or chafing his penis. And Amy notes that not every man appreciates her talents: "I've been with men who don't like it, I mean using it at all during intercourse. In that case I totally relax the muscle pressure and let him do all the thrusting, but at some point I'll start and we'll both go off—more sooner than later." Which hints at one common pitfall—lovers can get too excited: "Feels great—but be careful he doesn't go off too quick." "Sometimes you need to change the rhythm or knock it off completely—or else you can milk it right out of him. Men get extremely aroused."

Using the PC's is not a panacea; assuming she has normal muscle tone, a nonorgasmic woman will probably not become orgasmic by using PC exercises alone. We emphasize that three-quarters of the women in this study always require some degree of continuing clitoral stimulation. No woman stated that using her PC's was the crucial, commanding factor in her learning to be orgasmic. And many easily orgasmic women rarely make active use of their PC's—a matter of personal preference.

Nevertheless, all the above having been said, we hasten to add that the great majority of easily orgasmic women derive substantial benefit and pleasure from first exercising their PC muscles, then actively using them during sexual encounters. A woman can increase her acuteness of sensation, particularly during intercourse. She can elevate the intensity of, or prolong, her orgasm. Moreover, she has within her *own control* the means to add to sensation, to add to her totality of building erotic pleasure.

## *Genital Compatibility*

A woman rarely, if ever, measures her overall sexual (and emotional) satisfaction by the size of her lover's penis. A large —or medium or small—penis never substitutes for the quality of lover attached to it. For most women, penis size is unimportant:

*Julia:*
Penis size has no effect on how orgasmic I am. I was with a man within the last month who was small, but the way he entered me, his touching and technique—I came as much as always. Even when it's purely sex, it's more my attitude, whether I concentrate on what we're doing, on actively *making* love.

*Bernadette:*
Penis size is a man's hang-up. A man can have a small or medium-sized penis and be just great in bed. It's

like a man equating big breasts with sexiness in a
woman—I don't think breasts have anything to do
with being sexy or being good in bed. It's a stereotype.

Other women comment:

Perhaps unless your muscle tone is bad, it has no
bearing if you care about a person. Other abilities
matter more.

A penis itself is not arousing. How he caresses my
clitoris, how he pressures and rubs it in intercourse,
really is much more important.

It's basically meaningless. If he's not very big, I put a
pillow under my rear, or arch and raise myself for
deeper penetration. I adjust to what's there.

However, a substantial number of women, albeit a minority
of those we interviewed, *do* have some preferences about the
size of their lover's penis—and big isn't always better. Amy
observes: "It doesn't matter what size his penis is, but I only
hope that a man doesn't feel inadequate because of his size. A
lot of men feel, even say, 'Gee, I hope I can please you with
what I've got,' and it doesn't really matter to me. I've found
that men who are very small can be more pleasing than men
who are large. In fact, some men who are large are harder to
make love to because *they* feel inadequate—most of the women
they've dated have rejected them because they're large."
Indeed, some women do prefer a medium-size or "smaller"
penis:

I prefer a man who is smaller. I don't fear being hurt,
but a larger one is uncomfortable because I can't do as
much. In some positions it's hitting the back of my
vagina and, for me, that doesn't feel at all good.

A large one isn't good for me. I'm better able to reach
my special spot, my *clitoris*, with a small or medium or
even a semi-soft penis.

Men can sure get hung up on this, but frankly, for
physical—and maybe psychological—reasons, I don't
much like a large one. It can hurt.

A woman's preference can change over time, vary from partner to partner, or affect the way she makes love: "A large one
makes me climax faster, but it can get painful after a while. If
he's small, I need more concentration and I use a little of
everything—fantasy, position, activity. . . ."

And other women express a preference for a larger penis.
Sally is an artist, in her mid-forties, divorced, a trim, petite
woman who weighs 110 pounds: "I've given birth to five children. You know, they say that size doesn't make any difference
—but it makes a difference to me. Maybe I just never had
anyone big enough before my divorce, or maybe I have more
feeling because I've been exercising and stimulating my PC
muscles. Anyway, I like a big penis. The larger his penis, the
more my lover can stimulate me inside."

Here are additional comments:

Physically it doesn't matter to me—but it does
psychologically. A larger penis is mentally exciting.

No big deal, but I wouldn't say it's "unimportant,"
and I prefer thickness to length—not essential, but
nice.

My husband is large. To be honest with you, it *is*
important to me. A large penis is arousing.

"To be honest with you . . ." Several women were reluctant
to admit to a preference in penis size. Women may have several

reasons for their reluctance—perhaps they have read that all orgasms are triggered by clitoral stimulation, or that penis size shouldn't matter, or they feel that their preferences mark them as strange or lascivious, or they do not wish to be hurtful to a partner. However, we have seen that many women report areas of particular vaginal sensitivity. If the area is relatively "shallow," close to the vaginal entrance, a smaller, a medium-size, or even a thicker penis might most effectively and comfortably reach it; if the area is deep, a woman might desire a larger or a longer penis. Further, most women reach orgasm through a great totality of sensation, in which vaginal feelings may play an important role. Although, when a woman is aroused, her vagina is greatly "elastic," able to swell or compress to accommodate most any size penis, women still vary in their actual physical dimensions and their subjective feelings of vaginal size; some women feel their vagina is "large," others feel themselves "small." Circumvaginal muscle tone varies; thresholds of—or desires for—pain vary; psychological needs vary.

In any event, perhaps we might reconsider the wisdom of older cultures. For example, the Hindu *Kama Sutra* speaks of what may be termed "proper fit." A Very High Union is one where a couple's genital sizes are comparable in dimension; a Very Low Union results when a couple is greatly mismatched in genital dimension. Several women, in fact, spoke of a proper fit:

The size of his penis is sort of important. If he's too small, I can't feel him, but he certainly doesn't have to be huge. A nice match is best.

His caring and sensual abilities count most, but what you might call "fit" also counts. My fit is larger.

I'm small inside, and too large a penis is uncomfortable. Men have different shapes—long, short, thick, thin, straight, or bent—and how well we fit together matters. But most important is how well he uses whatever he has.

Let us not forget that penis size is truly unimportant to most women, and no woman wishes to fit her emotions, her relationship—or her lover—into a preconceived Procrustean bed of penis size. The great majority of men are endowed with an average-size penis which is perfectly pleasurable and adequate for the great majority of women. However, in reassuring men of this fact, therapists may also have unintentionally imparted a sense of inadequacy, guilt, or shame to the minority of women who do have definite preferences.

This and the previous two chapters have, primarily, dealt with the physical stimulations that bring an easily orgasmic woman near to the threshold of orgasm. Now we return to her mental arousal during lovemaking, the fascinating erotic world which rounds out her sexual activity.

# Pleasures of the Mind

Unless one reflects upon it, it's hard to realize how
much beautiful mental stuff goes on during lovemaking.

*—Kristin*

I have acquired a repertoire of movies in my mind.

*—Natalie*

M ind and body are one. In Chapter 4, "Starting on Warm,"
we likened a woman's mental activity to variations of
music. During lovemaking, while she absorbs the exquisite delights of mounting physical sensation, her mind responds and
creates, the music plays on and on. . . .

One woman explains, "You can't let anyone intimidate you
with his or their ideas of what you should think or feel. Believe
in yourself; believe in your own thoughts and feelings. The most
important thing I learned was letting my mind go free."

## Using All Your Senses

During lovemaking, a woman takes delight in a swarm of
sensory impressions. Aside from her pleasurable physical sensations, a woman gains mental excitement from being aware of
what she's doing—that she's losing her clothes, that she's taken
a lewd position, awareness that her lover is penetrating her
body. Place and circumstance can also be arousing, particularly
exotic vacation locales or sensually beautiful environments that
add to her acting out fantasies:

We've done it where I've always wanted to—like on
the beach, in bathrooms at parties, slyly at outdoor

concerts. But my favorite was in a private room at a very elegant restaurant, after a candlelight supper.

I gave him a lovely gift, and arranged for two massages —a woman for him and a man for me. Then two others, barely clothed, served us hors d'oeuvres and champagne. Then we petalled the roses, and scattered them over the bed. . . .

Acting out fantasies may sometimes include an element of the forbidden or the possibility of being discovered. Any such "adventurous" sex, including sex with a couple or a person recently met, or acting out a role or developing shared "scenarios," may add arousing thoughts to pleasing physical acts:

We take turns. Maybe he's the doctor and I'm his seductive patient, or maybe I'm his teacher and he's badly in need of discipline. Sometimes we'll dress the parts, and we'll probably play the scene until we've both reached climax. . . .

The actual visual experience of love is often highly arousing. The whole lovemaking scene can be a source of excitement, or a woman may prefer to notice particular visual aspects:

*Grace:*
Watching our bodies making love is amazingly arousing—and I'm not objective at all. Bodies are surprisingly sensual.

*Bernadette:*
It excites me to look at my breasts. The fact that we don't have clothes on, to see and feel him holding my breasts, to see my nipples erect.

*Rita:*
I look at my partner to feel more love and closeness. I

like to watch penetration, or his tongue between my
thighs. . . . It's also a turn-on to watch through
mirrors—I have two close to my bed. Because it
happens together, eye contact and feeling, sensations
are more intense.

Perhaps you will feel excitement from textures, tastes, or
scents: "I'm aroused by touch as a joy in itself, like textures,
warmth, my lover's skin, even breezes and water—anything
touching my body." Some women are highly aroused by sens-
ing taste and fragrance: "I love tastes and scents, and most of
all myself, my body smells and juices. I taste myself on his
fingers, and after we've had intercourse I like to do oral
love."
Or perhaps the sounds and words of love will reach you in
your genitals. Kristin says, "Words, cries, gurgles, and moans
are all communication—but they're also a turn-on, and a gift
to your lover."
Some women are extremely auditory during lovemaking.
Vivian, for example: "I like soft and romantic background
music. It helps heighten sensation—and drowns out my noises.
I love it when he says how terrific I am, or says, 'You're going
to get it.' I'm very vocal and I always have been . . . moans,
sighs, sometimes I scream, and sometimes I'll cry 'I'm coming!'
—all of it helps me let go."
Words of love and support, or spicy, sexy talk, or even a
downright dirty word may add to a woman's arousal:

My husband always says little things—how much he
loves me, how well-built I am, that he loves my nipples
and pussy. That helps me feel sexy.

I love to talk—how good it feels, how wet I am, "Do
it harder, faster," or "Look how you are glistening."
The words are stimulation, but I'm more aroused by
abandon, how free it feels to say them. And I want

my lover to share with me, to let me know *his* excitement.

I hear our noises and wet sounds, bodies making love. And I say, "You taste good," "I want to be fucked," "I'm wet, my breasts are growing." He can agree, like murmuring yes, but I don't want an "answer"—I'm talking to arouse myself.

He tells me stories, tells me I'm wet or hot. And it builds anticipation when he tells me what he'll do next, how I'll feel, what he'd *like* to do, even if it's some fantasy. And when I'm in the throes of passion, a few dirty words never hurt!

You may find, however, that your preference is silence: "In the beginning, I like to share passionate talk, but then I want only quiet sounds or silence—words disrupt my thoughts, and I'd rather be into sensations." "I don't like to hear myself and I try to be pretty quiet. Too much noise or talk distracts —and dirty words are a turnoff."
The pleasure derived from sounds and words is personal and varied; to help him turn you on, not off, express your tastes to your partner.

Many women are *mentally* aware of their state of physical arousal. Awareness is never detached, or a "watching" of one-self, but rather a subtle, fully involved immersion in bodily sensations. Arousal begets arousal:

I'm aware of my nipples, my lubrication, my clitoris and labia engorging, and I'm conscious of a rising feeling—I "tell myself" sensations.

I intensify sensations by cueing into feelings. It builds, warmer, stronger. I'm aware of my vaginal tension, my

whole body intensity. The more out of control I feel,
the more my arousal heightens.

Nora is aroused by anticipating feeling: "It's almost like I'm
waiting for a certain point and feeling. It's like a warning flag;
I'm actively thinking about that point, getting *excited* thinking,
because I know I'll be starting to roll—from then on I'm working on orgasm."

You may prefer to concentrate only on physical sensations,
to totally "blend" yourself with them far in advance of orgasm.

Kay is thirty-one, the manager of a housing development;
attractive strands of gray salt her dark brown hair. "To get to
orgasm, I have to focus on feelings. I empty my mind. I've had
some experience with yoga and hypnotism, and I enjoy meditat-
ing. When I'm making love I merge myself with every sensuous
feeling, whatever is pleasurably stimulated. Mind and body is
just all one, clitoris, anus, vagina, breasts—if the focus is on the
feet, *I'm* in the feet."

Few stimulations create more excitement than signs of a
lover's arousal. Many arousing sights and sounds signal a partner's enjoyment—his facial expressions, his noises of pleasure,
his words of praise and passion.

I feel good about myself, and it helps me get more
aroused, to know that I'm turning him on. I need
sensual feedback.

Getting to orgasm is a combination of my sensations
and perceiving his excitement. I get more aroused
myself if my lover's active and passionate. My
reactions as well, I'm sure, have an effect upon
him.

Feeling his arousal tells me I'm desired, and it helps
me to give up control. I also try to project myself and
get into his mind, what feels good to *him.*

Many women arouse *themselves* by "getting into" their partner's sensations. Kate explains, "I actually feel his sensations sometimes—and it's so exciting it scares me, like when he gets off on my breasts. He kisses and sucks them all over, wallows in them, tries to put it all in his mouth, and he's getting so damn excited that *I* can almost get off. Maybe my breasts had been sensitive, but all of a sudden there's no more pain—I'm so much into his feelings that I can't get them enough."

A woman can use all her senses to increase sexual arousal. Focus only on stimuli that bring you closer to orgasm—and give yourself the freedom to do your part in creating them.

## A Very Private Affair

Now we enter the fascinating realm of a woman's thoughts and images.

A partner is usually unaware of a woman's mental activity, and indeed it is her prerogative to keep him unenlightened. As one woman declares, "It's *my* business." Sometimes telling a fantasy as it unfolds or arises can greatly enhance excitement, but frequently, particularly during lovemaking, communication disrupts concentration or lessens the sexual impact of a favorite thought or image.

It often takes time to freely accept mental images. Iris recalls, "Within the past year I have realized why a couple of times I've stopped myself and haven't come to orgasm—because I'm thinking, 'Hey, wait a minute! I'm with this guy but I'm seeing this stranger!' But then I decided that's part of making love— everybody has fantasies." And Bernadette: "It took me a while to feel comfortable, to accept them as normal and feminine, but then I found that fantasy has a lot to do with sex."

However, some highly orgasmic women have always used mental images. Victoria, twenty-eight, has moderate muscular dystrophy. An art therapist, she is a single, slender woman with abundant honey-brown hair: "I need a mental image during lovemaking, and I'm distracted if my partner's not in tune with it. I try one after another until one turns me on. I don't think I've ever had an orgasm by just trying to feel physical sensations."

Images come and go. At one moment a woman may totally merge herself with physical sensations; at another, her mind may absorb only images; at still another, image and sensation combine in one exciting experience. Imaging can be similar to cinematic technique: slow motion, intercuts, zooms in and out. The degree of realism can vary, from impressionistic to highly abstract to detailed and realistic. And most women harbor preferences for specific techniques of imaging, as well as for a sensory mode—visual, kinesthetic, or auditory—which normally aids her arousal.

The mode a woman prefers is difficult to predict. For example, Emily was trained as a graphic artist and worked in that field for years, yet she images in the feeling mode—and cannot conjure up any visuals: "It's just not my style. I've tried and it just doesn't work." Wendy is also an artist: "I project a lot, let myself become very sensitive. If an image is in my mind and it isn't of another person, it might be of a painting or something, I don't just toss it off and think about the person. I wouldn't really say I have fantasies. If I close my eyes and see myself in a sea of rich velvet purple, I get off on the purple. I imagine what the color feels like, and my skin gets sensitive from that. I'm a visual thinker, I was trained in that in art school. I give life to all my images."

Although Wendy's natural—or trained—predilection is for visual images, she tightly integrates image with sensation. We cannot emphasize that enough. Whatever a woman's preference, her mind is not off and scattered. Ultimately, to reach the peak of orgasm, she translates mental excitement into sexual physical pleasure. Meredith further explains, "I see abstract things, spirals, colors, and waves, or even stroking hands—and I'll feel them. Things float in that I can't describe, but it's really the *feelings* I'm after."

Content arousing to one woman may well be rejected by another: "I see lots of abstract pictures, but I don't have whore-ish images, or thoughts like 'His cock is harder.' " "I don't like to 'watch' us make love in my mind because I don't feel in-volved—but I do love images of penises!"

Joan, blond and vivacious, is an actress in her late twenties. Married, born and raised in the South, she comes from "a *very* fundamentalist, Southern Christian" background: "My rela-tionship with God touches all aspects of life. . . . I've read so much about fantasizing other situations or people, yet I don't understand the connection. I feel it would take from the mo-ment, the relationship, like extricating myself too much or being completely selfish. You're not giving your mind and thoughts . . . like cheating the other person." During lovemak-ing, Joan might see an image of herself acting a role, then switch to a mental "long shot" of her husband and her making love, and then see close-up images of her sexual body parts. These images heighten arousal, and yet preserve Joan's loyalty, a value she highly prizes.

## Fantasy

Hillary is in her late thirties, a striking, darkly exotic woman who seems to radiate energy as she tells of her fantasy: "I always have this fantasy when I'm riding on top of my husband, some type of horse fantasy, and when it's in my mind, it stays with me all night. I'm completely naked and, bareback, I'm riding this beautiful stallion and it's like there's a whole herd of horses behind me. I don't particularly look like myself, and though I'm not that way in real life, in my fantasy I'm a wild, dominating woman. In the vague background of the scene—I'm riding toward them—are always these very strong men, admiring how I'm dominating the horses. I sense they're waiting to take me, to have sex with me, but somehow I know I would dominate them—I've got full control, my own power and the horses' power, power is all on my side. I'm always in a dominant position in this, and I'm riding hard, pressing down . . . riding it almost to orgasm."

All internal images, even visual images, are not necessarily "fantasy." Many women do not consider their images to be fantasy. Witness Wendy, immersed in a sea of rich velvet purple: "I wouldn't really say I have fantasies." And fantasy carries negative connotations for many women, implying "removal" from her actual partner, whereas many images are partner-bound and relate to the woman's body or the immediate sexual activity. Finally, the term "fantasy," used as a broad and inclusive description, does not convey the diversity of rich, inventive images employed by many women. "Fantasy" is a term we reserve for extended internal images of the woman herself and/or other persons engaging in some activity, usually including some features of the environment. As in Hillary's fantasy, a feature or two may be pronounced, while several are vague or intuited.

Very often, fantasies (and other images) are "Remembrances of Things Past," reconstructions based upon actual past experiences. A woman may recall a particularly tender or arousing moment, or an exciting or relaxing locale or circumstance. She may conceive of her image as entirely visual, or use the visual cue to resurrect past sensations. Here is one woman's fantasy, arising during lovemaking, which reaches directly for feeling: "A certain movement or look—and then it will flash, 'We were like this before.' To a point I relive it, try to recapture the environment of when we were on the beach, the peaceful climate and warmth, yet it's not like I'm watching movies in my head, but a *feeling* that flows through my body."

Some women frequently or exclusively image the partner

with whom they are making love, or always include him in scenes involving others, or "switch" to him as the scene unfolds. And fantasy arises not only because a woman consciously "needs" or desires extra stimulation; for women like Ingrid, the greater her lovemaking pleasure, the more abundant her fantasies: "If I needed to conjure up pictures to get a good feeling, I would have no problem doing it. But usually if it's great, if I'm really enjoying our making love, it more reminds me of great times we've had, and scenes just come by themselves."

Other past partners may come to mind. This often occurs when a woman is having difficulty becoming aroused—but not always: "When my husband suggests fantasies, like making love with friends or movie stars, it also invites some memories of wonderful lovers I've had." Fantasies may also recall past acted fantasies, or even a past, fleeting event that still evokes arousal: "I get flashes of a pornographic picture that I saw—like years ago, when I was in eighth grade. A kid showed it to me. There was a circle of people—man, woman, man, woman—and each man had his hands on the next woman's breasts, and each woman had her hands on the next man's penis. It still comes to mind sometimes while I'm making love."

Fantasies also freely express a woman's erotic desires, fancied sensations and acts or things she might like to do, and many fantasies group around themes, such as The Tender Seduction: "I see it how I want it. Even though the actual is faster, I visualize a slow making love, with lots of soft, gentle touches." "I see this all the time, seduction. A man slowly undressing me, taking off my bra, easing down my panties. . . . We go all the way, and I actually feel penetration."

Another common theme is The Vague or Handsome Stranger. He has many advantages. He can be everything a woman desires, and without the drawbacks, realities, or guilts attached to specific persons: "I don't see an exact person but a stranger. They're very muscular, usually have dark hair, and he's making love on top of me. His face is usually blank—that's why I guess he's a stranger." "It's like a chance meeting and I leave with them. They're like vague strangers, bodies without faces, and they please me however I wish."

Women often fantasize making love with a friend, acquaintance, or even a specific stranger—"I can think of someone I saw that night in a restaurant." Many women visualize themselves with famous personalities. Succeeding generations admire changing "symbols"; rock music stars, for example, or television and film celebrities. And characters from movies and books often make excellent lovers; a woman replaces "the female" or adds herself as a character in lurid or sensual scenes. Frequently, the scene is merely a starting point—she further develops the action wherever her urges lead her, usually "toward romance" or "being ardently taken."

If one fantasy lover is good, several may be better—more admiration and lust, more helpless submission, more sheer physical pleasure: "Men want me, but lovingly, romantically. I'm holding my hands back, giving in, my legs slowly spread open. . . ." "I'm at a resort or another city. Several men and a woman pick me up and make love to me. . . ." Fantasies of trios or groups recur with marked regularity, as does the prevalent fantasy of making love to a woman: "My lesbian fantasy —three women arousing me, all there for my pleasure . . ." "I'm alone with a woman in her bedroom, both of us gentle, soft and caressing, enjoying oral love. . . ."

As well as becoming part of a scene, being there and watching can also provide stimulation: "In romance books, when the man and woman first meet, there's always a clash. They can't get along—and then he grabs her. That's the point, when I'm making love, when I'll put myself right in and watch, feeling whatever they feel." Usually, however, being watched by others is more powerful than watching: "I've been captured by a group of men and the leader of the pack—my husband—is having his way while I'm constrained. The others are watching . . . the threat is there that he'll let them have me." Other "watching" fantasies are a husband watching a woman making love to his friends, other men watching her make love to her husband, and watching a husband make love to other women.

Finally, an extremely common fantasy is being "forced" to submit: "I have this fantasy of being overpowered—'rape,' but not rape really. I'm being made to do and enjoy things I'd not do otherwise." "I'm almost like a shy virgin, made to have dirty sex." "My husband invites his friends to dinner and he makes me serve them almost nude, dressed in a skimpy costume. They touch me as I pass, and I do oral love . . . then all together they take me." Occasionally the fantasy reverses: "I have a great turn-on fantasy of rendering him totally helpless, then doing whatever I want to—and I'll really do it someday!"

Often, keen, specifically sexual sensations—breast, clitoral, and vaginal—are attached to a woman's fantasies. Eighty percent of the women in our study, at least on occasion, and within our narrow definition, fantasize during lovemaking.

## Going With Roles and Moods

Mimi relates, "I'm a performer, and I know how to develop personalities. A lot of sex is mind-set for me, and I tend to be more glamorous and sensual when I'm doing my roles in a sexual experience. But I don't 'act like' these women, I'm bringing out the parts of me embodied in them, allowing myself to explore the different aspects of who I am, and I can be more creative and uninhibited. I have certain roles where I let myself go—I don't hold back in theater—and if I think 'Be like Nedda,' I'm giving myself permission. Nedda is from *Pagliacci,* the very sexy wife, and I once had a sexy leading man—I was *steaming* on stage every night! So while I'm making love, I also mentally see myself and often see a role—the sexy and abandoned things I may desire to do, the uninhibited, sensual things we're actually, physically doing."

As in fantasies, certain themes recur in moods and in acted or imaged roles. Naturally, many women enjoy a diverse repertoire of arousing moods and roles; the sweet, innocent girl of tonight might feel like a hooker tomorrow. And roles resist strict "categories," often overlapping; nonetheless, we will point up some themes that foster a woman's arousal. You may encounter a facet of your own personality—or give yourself permission to use your creative powers.

During lovemaking, a majority of the women have either acted the roles or felt the moods of dominance and/or submission. These strains flavor other roles and serve as the central catalyst of many acts and fantasies. Perhaps these urges represent an eternal struggle between the sexes, and surely they express emotions that linger in all of us. Healthy, creative people often engage in playful forms of dominance and submission. In tune with a partner's mood, enjoyed with consideration, expressing the feelings of dominance/submission may greatly enhance arousal.

Some women always prefer one or the other mood, consistently acting or feeling dominant or submissive. However, most women who have these feelings tend to have them both—at one moment dominant, at another softly submissive: "When I'm feeling dominant, I'm likely to dress in black and leather. I'm more in control and aggressive, and think about or give orders. I visualize myself as powerful and strong. That's my more natural role. But then I can feel submissive, see myself as passive, and lie back and close my eyes or grab on to the bedstead, or struggle until he takes me."

A substantial minority of the women, at least on occasion, have been mentally and physically aroused by being placed in bondage, and half of these women reverse the role by also restraining their partners. The psychic and physical pleasures vary with every woman: "I like the feeling of helplessness, of being *given* an orgasm, of being able to focus myself entirely on sensations." "I feel I must surrender, and his making decisions

for me gives me the feeling he's caring." "I like the feeling of
no control, of never knowing in advance what he will do to my
body. The height of a sexual peak in restraint is—oh, maybe ten
times greater than normal." However, several women had tried
bondage, and stopped: "I hated it, felt panic and phobia without
free hands." "It was nothing. I'd rather be able to move." "It
was *too* hot, too arousing to feel comfortable."

Many other women physically simulate bondage: "He holds
my hands under me." "I act as if my hands were tied." Victoria
notes: "I love to act out a gentle rape fantasy, like when I hold
my hands over my head, pressed against the bed. But I have to
be careful that my rape scenario 'Stop' sounds different from
my real *'Stop!'* " And Grace explains: "I've had my hands
under his and I've done the same to him, that kind of thing—
I like sensual dominance. But in the real world, I detest rape
or force."

Though many women are highly aroused by thoughts or
fantasies of bondage, the *great majority* of women have no
desire to act them out.

Various roles represent The Good, Sweet Innocent Girl. In
this mood or role, a woman often desires seduction—and les-
sons on how to make love: "I'm a sweet, innocent little girl, and
act like he's the first man I've seen in maybe months or years
—and then I just relax. . . ." "The thought comes in by itself:
'I'm a virgin, I've never done this before.' But I'm nice, cuddly,
and willing—and usually on the bottom." However, the role of
Naughty Seductress is somewhat more common than "Sweet."
Presumably, it affords greater latitude for uninhibited sex: "I
become a sexy 'bad' girl, seductive, alluring, and wicked—and
maybe a little bit whoreish. I want raw sex, more roughness,
and I'm willing to do most everything." "When I wear stockings and garter belts, I think of myself as naughty but nice, as
being an exhibitionist." "In the everyday world, people think
I'm innocent and sweet. But often, while making love, I have

this secret, arousing thought—how bad and naughty I am, how shocked they'd be at my secret life."

A woman may also feel glamorous: "When I'm aroused, I can suddenly feel beautiful and sexy—and it *is* really an inner me, who I have become." Or she may become, in her image, a glamorous model or actress, or transform herself to a knockout whom men find irresistible. Constance relates her concept: "It's the psyching up, the getting ready—imagining I'm the greatest lover, super sexy, a man can't say no. I picture myself voluptuous, a naked, attractive woman, walking toward a man and I know I will give him pleasure. My carriage is almost aloof, like 'Come to me if you dare,' and I know he'll reach to grab me —but it never gets to that sequence. And it's not constant—I'm too involved with making love—but it flashes in and out." Coral has a similar image: "Sometimes I see both of us, but I'm very much the focus. I'm terribly powerful, an irresistible goddess drawing my lover to me, and I also might see him in this way—not every partner, certainly—but I make him like a god, worthy of my attention. I conjure it just for a moment and know when I'm doing it, and say to myself, 'Well, it's all right, it's just that I deserve this!' "

And several women imaged the role of Earth Mother or Primeval Woman. Grace's concept is elegant: "If my mood is primitive, I see us making love in a cave, but always on a fur rug. And there's a skylight—the sky represents few restrictions. Everything is soft and round, without rigid control, and my cave affects the way I make love, more like a hungry tigress." Erica's role is entirely internal, and more symbolic or cosmic: "I think to myself, 'My God, what a woman can do,' or 'My God, what a woman has between her legs,' or 'This is an awesome power.' It makes the earth move, keeps the species going. 'Motherhood' sounds sentimental, but I think about myself as a procreative being. And I see myself on the earth, lying in that position, and sense my power, my largeness on the landscape. This is where I come from and this is what I'm supposed to be.

Things are coming together now. I'm a woman. My back is on the earth. A primal image goes way back, this is like the beginning. In that very position, in such a moment far, far before orgasm, I will maybe think 'Adam and Eve-ish,' without any fall, without emotional sin attached but in terms of the first creation. And what are these powers and what are these forces that bring us together? I feel more adult, older. I don't feel like just a student, or my mother's little girl. Hey, I'm a woman and I'm doing my thing."

Of course, there's a partner on the receiving end of all these roles and thematic moods. What happens when he ignores, rejects, or misreads the moods, or has a mood of his own? Kate cautions, "With someone you really don't know well, you have to be very careful. You don't know what's going to backfire, or what his reaction will be. He might say 'You slut!' because I'm too strong or sexy, and I want to be able to handle whatever comes my way."

Most women are flexible, able to change their roles and moods to meet the situation. However, a woman is usually more orgasmic, and finds lovemaking more satisfactory, when a lover knows of or senses her mood, and then accepts or embraces it. When moods or roles conflict, "whoever's is strongest" usually wins out, and sometimes conflict in roles provides exciting drama. Many women, such as Michelle, relish the situation when both she and her partner yen for the feeling of dominance: "It depends on the level of dominance. Sometimes he wins out, sometimes I do—but it's always a beautiful fight to the finish!"

Occasionally, when a role is especially important to a woman, its rejection by a partner can leave her feeling dissatisfied, and possibly nonorgasmic. Rita: "Outwardly, in the world, I can adapt myself very easily. But making love, when my role is ignored or rejected, I end up feeling that something is missing. The sex might still be good, but sometimes I'll only lie there and think, 'When will it be over?' " And other women: "If I need to change, it messes me up. It's hard to feel passive, and then need to switch." "If he doesn't respond to my mood or role, I might turn off or be angry—but good, sensitive lovers like to get into my head space."

Rigid adherence to, and need for, a role is not to be encouraged, yet women—and their caring partners—should know that freely expressing a mood will add to sexual pleasure.

Ninety percent of the women in this study, at least on occasion, use thematic moods or acted or imaged roles to heighten their sexual arousal.

## Silent Words

Vivian is highly aroused by audible, erotic sounds and words, and orgasmic through spoken suggestion. She also heightens sensation by "hearing" the silent words of her own mind's creation: "I tell myself what sensations I'm feeling, especially closer to orgasm. Sometimes they're sounds or thoughts, other times actual words. I think 'beautiful,' 'growing,' or John might ask me how I feel and I respond in my mind: 'Fantastic, wonderful!' Maybe the words excite me by focusing my sensations."

Silent words or phrases, even extensive dialogues, often accompany fantasies and roles. They also exist by themselves as sources of stimulation, a resource totally subject to a woman's own control.

If I'm with a partner who doesn't talk, doesn't verbally communicate, I won't say anything to him, but I'll sometimes do it in my mind. I can hear him saying what I'd like him to say, or say what I'd like to tell him.

Words go through my head a lot, and sometimes it seems like I'm saying them aloud though usually I'm really not. Complimentary words, or things about what feels good. Like "More" or "Faster," or maybe most common, "I love you."

I'm conscious of them, emotional, positive thoughts which help keep in touch with sensations. "Move his hand here," or "Why don't you put your hand there?" or "I'm passionate and hot." And then I know sensations I want and concentrate on that feeling. It's like, "Yeah, that's the feeling! That's the one I want! We're onto it!"

Silent words are often used when a woman feels unexcited: "I tell myself, 'Look, orgasm doesn't matter. He's a very nice person, so just enjoy each instant, these nice sensations, the play, the pleasure we're giving each other.' And then I do what I've thought—and usually before I know it, I'm almost ready to come." However, there is also a downside to silent words. Two women found themselves counting during sex, usually during intercourse when they were positioned on their backs, and when they were bored or inactive—and also not orgasmic. Silent counting seems a sure sign that it's time to move your body and get your mind on sex.

Though silent words usually increase arousal by giving vent to exciting thoughts, a very orgasmic woman, like Tina, can use them to hold back her climax: "What I concentrate on, at times, is not having an orgasm. If I keep myself from having an orgasm until I can't stand it anymore, it's much more intense and complete. There are times when it's one or two minutes— and boom! I'll sacrifice multiples for one nice biggie. The excitement level's there, usually in oral sex, and it's like keeping the level lower, keeping sensation away. I move back a little bit, then up a little bit, and back and think some more . . . 'I don't want to come, I don't want to come . . .' until I can't help going."

For one woman in our study, an auditory image is her primary means of mental arousal. Heather is in her mid-thirties, from a Methodist family background. Rangy yet solidly built, she is somewhat demure in demeanor. She describes her auditory image as "stronger" and more arousing than any of her visual images, and states that it "always" occurs whenever she's making love: "A lot of it is verbal, like a narrator talking and explaining what's happening. When I'm making love with someone, a voice describes to someone else the sexual things we're doing, like whispering in my ear, yet he's not talking to me. And he doesn't know my body reactions, it's more like he's describing what's happening in front of him. And it's not porno language, but more a normal conversation, the type of language I'd use myself—after all, I *do* it myself, so the man says what I want: 'He's entering her now,' 'She's doing it,' 'He's thrusting into her,' 'Oh, oh, there she is, getting ready to come!' "

## *I Am a Camera: Third-Person Observer Images*

Among easily orgasmic women, we discovered two types of images, the prevalence of which has largely escaped popular and professional notice. These images are rooted in the ongoing moment of lovemaking—a woman's sexual activities with her partner and the sexual responses of her body. As such, they are not only highly arousing, but entirely faithful to the moment and a woman's partner relationship.

We term one of these images a *third-person observer image.* A *majority* of the women report this erotic experience. As if she were a movie camera, or another person watching, a woman has varied images of what she and her partner are actually, sexually doing, though some women change it a bit or add a touch of fantasy. However, an orgasmic woman is never detached, never a passive "spectator," aloof from her sexual experience—detachment often characterizes *non* orgasmic women. Although aware of the image, her own and/or her lover's excited, ardent caresses, orgasmic women remain immersed in simultaneous sensations. Further, arousal is usually much more intense when a woman senses or feels herself as being *within* the picture, and not on a distant planet.

A few women, like Lisa, consistently conjure these images: "It's in my mind, like a mirror on the ceiling, and I *always*, at least for some moments, see myself making love."

*Ginger:*
Sometimes I'm like a third person, watching myself from out of the bed. I see what I'm actually doing, like my own body on top or rear penetration—and yet my focus is always on me, for my own sexual pleasure, and I'm absolutely feeling everything that's happening.

*Rita:*
What I see are bodies. Like during oral sex—and it might not even be exactly what is happening—I see my body stretched out on a bed and a man's body kneeling by mine. My legs are probably up, and my hands are along the sides of his head. It's just the image and feelings, a very soft, very beautiful image. And I see the body movements but I don't see the details . . . just the scene, very soft lights and images and me. . . .

Some women see the image as if in a slow-motion movie or dream. The image may also anticipate desired, arousing sensations, or include sounds and words:

*Michelle:*
I don't think I try, it just happens—realistic pictures of my partner and I making love. Like side-angle shots or views from the top. If I move my hand over him, I may see a shot of my hand coming over his body . . . and it's usually like a slow-motion film, very slow and dreamy.

*Ingrid:*
I see it in my mind as a slow-motion movie unfolding,
what we're doing and hearing—everything goes in it.
Although I'm being aroused, I'm not seeing me as
much as watching my husband make love. I feel what
he's already done or what he's going to do next, see
and feel it coming, embellish it in my mind. . . .

*Willa is in her forties, tall, willowy, black; she possesses
an infectious ebullience—and a laugh to coax smiles
from stone:*
I see that all the time! Like I'm looking from outside
myself and seeing what's going on! And I hear what
we're saying, both of us—with a few extra words
thrown in. I can see myself now, on top, teasing him,
in control. . . .

As Willa throws in a few extra words, many women mentally
add some extra stimulation:

*Kristin:*
Watching can be arousing if I let my head get into it. I
normally see what we're doing, but I sometimes add a
man, never someone I know but always a shadowy
presence. I usually see the classic, a man screwing me
from the front while another screws from the rear. My
lover's entering vaginally, and I add an anal entry.

*Darcie:*
I see us both making love, but I sometimes end up
changing it—and almost feel what I picture. My
favorite is adding a person—someone else joins in. Like
during oral or intercourse, he or she goes down on me
or kisses and touches my breasts.

*Natalie:*
I've always done it, sort of watched what we're doing
that moment. And I can add men—never women—and

be aware who they are. Yet I never imagine their faces
but mainly parts of their bodies, like abdomens, rear
ends, and thighs—and mostly extra hands. Hands
become large, I see fine details like their nails . . .
hands inside my vagina, touching my nipples, my
clitoris, bottom . . . hands all over my body. Maybe
that's how I have breast orgasms, imagining lots of
sensations.

These third-person observer images blend toward a different
type of image, those of specific body parts. Peg, who is ultra
orgasmic, states: "I see everything in my mind's eye, all our
acts, all our fantasies and roles, whatever positions we're in
. . . and then more and more my body . . . my clitoris, my vagina
. . . and then I become sensation." Among women who have
visual images, there seems a progression during lovemaking,
a tendency to move toward body-part images the closer a woman nears orgasm. Occasionally, a woman will take a fantasy or
role image right through the peak of orgasm, but more frequently, as erotic arousal mounts, her focus begins to shift toward third-person and body-part images . . . closer to pure
sensation.

## Body-Part Imaging

The prevalence of *body-part imaging* among easily orgasmic
women is an unexpected discovery. We have not encountered
a comprehensive description of such imaging in either the popular or professional literature. A *substantial majority* of women
in our study frequently have these images. We say frequently
because a woman who is aware of having one of these images
usually has many. And we suspect that the actual incidence is
greater than that uncovered by our interviews: Many of these
images are fleeting impressions, and quickly forgotten after
lovemaking.

What do we mean by body-part imaging? Simply, a woman will have close-up images, usually visual, of her own body parts or her partner's while she is making love. These images are felt to be "natural," usually spontaneous, extremely arousing—and, for several women, nearly essential to orgasm:

*Ursula, when asked if she ever visualizes body parts or areas while making love:*
You mean other people don't?

*Jennifer is twenty-one and single, a recent college graduate:*
I think that's terribly important, just visualizing my clitoris or the parts of my body being touched, and as a result, experiencing all the *feelings* from it. That helps me a lot for orgasm.

*Iris:*
I very definitely see images of my body as it's aroused. I think that's a necessity, very important. You have to realize yourself, your body parts, how each part feels to you when it's being touched. To come to an orgasm, I enjoy a multiple amount of stimulation.

Although most body-part images have a visual component, some are purely kinesthetic, a recall or recognition of arousing bodily feelings. Tracy, who has a visual orgasmic image, images only sensation during her arousal: "Something might cue a memory, and past sensations pop in." And Emily, who never has visual images, relates: "My first orgasm was shocking. It kind of scared me, but I knew right away I liked it. Then I got worried that it wasn't going to happen again. So I touched myself more and went back in my mind through the entire sexual experience to see what made me feel good, trying to capture whatever sensations I went through. Now I think about how I'm feeling and concentrate where he's touching. I can help control it . . . I'm familiar with the feelings of arousal."

What does a woman see when she visually images body parts? Let us try to fathom the scope of one woman's experience. Grace is aware of her images: "I'm a visual and tactile person. I watch our loveplay [third-person images], but later on I see areas. I see my husband clearly—I'm a chest, shoulders, and butt woman—or his genitals, face, mouth, or tongue, his head between my legs. But I see myself as a vaguer form, and especially where there's feeling, like his mouth upon my breast. Then I see my nipples, my pelvis, clitoris, thighs—and particularly my vagina. I focus on vaginal insertion. As if I'm inside my vagina, I see his penis start to descend as if it were coming toward me. I only sense my vaginal walls, but his penis is hard and powerful. I see and feel it ripple and glide, and when he impacts the cervix, I have automatic pictures, and can actually feel like the cervix. This sounds weird, but I always see it. You know how you do a radish, and use this thing to flip petals down? When I'm feeling the gliding and impact, I feel very pink and open . . . like puffy, beige-colored tissue . . . somehow plushly open at the same time I'm drawing in . . . like a plum or that kind of shape, feeling good sensations. . . ."

Kristin relates, "I can see my nipples and clitoris swelling, getting larger and harder, and my lubricating vagina. . . ." And Ursula: "I see my vulva enlarging, realistic swollen lips of a reddish-purple-blue color." To reach her own orgasm, Tina shifts her focus from her partner to herself: "When I want to come, I imagine myself and not him. I sometimes see my vagina moving, my labia slowly becoming engorged, slowly spreading open. . . ."

Most body-part images are visualizations of contact, both the woman's and partner's parts in felt and seen combinations. Realistic or somewhat abstract, representing a woman's vision of what their bodies might look like, the images have an extremely strong link to felt, immediate sensations: "I visualize on sensations." "I see what feels intense or arousing." A common image is the penis within the vagina, usually seen as a cutaway view, "from the side, like looking through a window." Others see it as Grace does, especially when the man is on top—"I'm at the very bottom point and see the penis coming"—or see it as a man might: "If my mood is lust, I see my legs spread, and a view from behind his penis, plunging in my vagina." Every arousing caress may be visualized: a hand, fingers, mouth, or tongue upon a woman's mouth or breast, her skin, nipples, labia, clitoris, buttocks, anus, vagina. Her own caresses: a penis within her mouth, a hand or tongue on his body, her circum-vaginal muscles closing upon his penis.

Many women image ejaculation: "I see his penis throbbing, then spurting inside my vagina." However, even before they touch, a woman may see her partner's parts, particularly his penis, or face, chest, hands—whatever she may value as erotic stimulation. For Cynthia, thirty-two and married, her image is almost a symbol, personifying the "best" of a sometimes diffi-cult husband: "When we're making love, I visualize his back. He's very big and strong, and it seems like all of him, his overall person, his personality. Even though he drinks, he's such a fantastic person. His back is all good, warm, caring, secure, and nicely, sexually arousing. It's not like he's on the phone, saying how much he loves me. He's *here.*"

Sometimes a woman's images "alter" stimulations: "I feel nipple sensations, and imagine his hand or mouth there." "His mouth, sucking my nipples, can transfer to an image of his lips upon my clitoris." Or, to enhance arousal, a woman may image her body as a personal or cultural "ideal." Natalie relates, "In my mind my breasts are sometimes larger than most breasts ever get! It becomes a very Freudian, nursing type thing." And Willa tells of a similar experience: "I was taught that skinny was awful, and I always wanted to be a size twelve. When I make love, I visualize his hand moving on my breast—except it's always bigger than my breast really is! When I see my body, it's made a little better. My partner might be caressing my thighs or doing oral sex—and I might just see my hips. They're nice! Mine, but bigger and round."

A woman may also anticipate desired stimulations. Alice is

in her late twenties, from a Catholic family background. She is single, working on a master's, and has long, golden hair: "During oral sex, I sometimes jump ahead in my mind and see myself in intercourse. If I'm going to peak it, especially if I've had one orgasm and the same tongue or kissing is building toward another, I'll let my partner know that I feel an urge to have intercourse. I often see quick side views of his penis inside my vagina. When I need deeper thrusting, it helps me establish a rhythm, and to know how to move him to get where it feels good."

Using body-part imaging, Brenda, thirty-one and married for thirteen years, taught herself to be orgasmic from oral stimulation. She had been orgasmic in intercourse, yet shied away from oral sex until she decided to "learn it," employing her *own* conceptions (which reflect her personal sensations) of how her body functioned: "First I had to understand the mechanics. I did a little reading, and more or less formed a picture of how my body became aroused and touched off into climax. The way I understood it, the veins and arteries around the uterine cavity fill up with blood, the same as a penis does. That build-up is the arousal, like the sensation of a climax growing to the top of a mountain. And then at the top, at the release of orgasm, all those arteries and veins open up and that blood releases back. Once I understood that, I had to think of a way to get there. I realized I could see that happening in my head, and once I could see it, I would know what to expect. It's like a moving picture: I see the uterus and I see an outer aura, and then as intensity builds I see the aura swelling, as if it's fueling the uterus, expanding almost to bursting—and then all of a sudden the bursting point just happens . . . and it's like a soft balloon, collapsing into my body.

"I don't have to think about it now, but in the beginning, when I started wanting to become successful at oral love, and I learned the process, imagining the build-up was a big factor in achieving it."

A woman's imaging usually stops in the moments just before orgasm—or a new type of image is initiated. Yet a few women do experience "comprehensive" or related images that start in mid-arousal and extend through the peak of orgasm. Natalie is such a woman, possessing, as she alerted us, a "repertoire" of images, and some are of special beauty:

"When I'm having oral sex, I see all the little creases and crevices in my vagina, my clitoris as large and swollen and enlarging even more, and fluttering, because it usually does before and after orgasm. . . . When he enters initially, I have an image of this large, beautiful penis perfectly filling a marvelous space, an incredible feeling to have something in you, enter inside your body, a very romantic feeling that now we have united. . . . The walls of my vagina are rather narrow and long, very realistic, pink, fleshy, and moist. . . . When he comes inside me, I feel a flush of warm, ivory liquid and watch it coming towards me, very gently and lightly washing over my presence. . . .

"When I am ready for orgasm, I have always imagined my vagina as being doors opening and closing. . . . The doors are deep inside me, surrounded by fleshy vagina. They open like double French doors, white, very delicate, feminine. I see them slowly opening, then staying open at orgasm. Sometimes, depending how wet I am, I see blue water seep out the doors, as if that's the way I'm coming. Then, as I'm done, after I've had my orgasm, I see the doors slowly closing. . . ."

Of the easily orgasmic women in our study, *80 percent,* at least on occasion, have third-person observer and/or body-part images.

## Nourishing Orgasm

Though orgasm is "physical," taking place in the body, orgasmic women use their minds to nourish their bodies to orgasm.

For a few women, this nourishment takes the form of a simple focusing in, concentrating their minds to blending with pure sensation. But most do immensely more: She pre-arouses her body and mind before a sexual encounter; she focuses in on making love, eliminating distractions; she uses all her senses, choosing, and also creating, erotic sensory input. Including preparatory imaging, fifty-nine of the sixty women create some form of erotic imaging. During lovemaking, 90 percent sometimes use a form of visual imaging; 80 percent have fantasies; 90 percent use roles or go with thematic moods; 80 percent use third-person views or close-up body-part images. When all these factors are added, the total effect is striking: *Orgasmic women make doubly sure of enough stimulation for orgasm.*

However, *no* woman does everything. As Grace, who focuses on images and sensory impressions and is always immersed in her body's sensations, exclaims: "I can't have fantasies too— there's just no more mental room!" Indeed there is not. At any given moment, a person can engage in only so much mental activity. Further, women have preferences; each attends to whatever, for her, is most erotically pleasing. One attends to pure sensation, aided perhaps by a feeling image or boosted by audible input. Another sees vivid images, another acts roles or fantasies. . . . There are infinite possibilities, and therefore infinite choices. Only you can choose.

# 10

# Orgasm

Something that final, that comfortable, that warm and good, has to be something worth having.

—*Harriet*

As the final moment approaches, a woman tends to focus on her most outstanding sensations. Whether they're in her clitoris or deep within her vagina, or both, her body cries for more and more of these marvelous sensations. . . . "For heaven's sake don't stop! Don't change a thing!"

A woman means that literally. A strong, unanimous fact swiftly emerged from our study: What a woman needs at this moment is steady, *reliable* stimulation, a final, steady—occasionally increased—tactile rhythm and pressure:

*Mimi:*
Yes, yes, yes, it has to be the same thing for maybe fifteen or thirty seconds before I get an orgasm. If somebody changes a thing—we start all over again.

*Tina:*
At the end, I only need five or ten seconds of steady stimulation, but if I'm right there and he changes what he's doing, it always removes the intensity—and maybe blows the whole thing.

*Erica:*
Maybe thirty seconds is about right. To give me something constant and sure, so then I can do my own thing.

*Vivian:*
I need maybe thirty seconds, more if I'm not too much
in the mood—and oh yes, yes, a change can always kill
it. And pressure and rhythm go very much together—
both are needed to make it.

*Paula:*
Definitely, definitely, yes, rhythm, motion, hardness,
fastness . . . whatever it is, it has to be the same. Same
everything, don't move a hair!

*Rachel:*
I need about ten or twenty seconds, sort of coinciding
with the early spasms I feel. If he stops, I'm really
turned off—if he stops or changes, I'll *kill him!*

*And the irrepressible Dorothy:*
For probably thirty seconds, if one thing changes, I
lose it. You know what really gets me? When you're
with somebody for the first time, and they find the spot
and you're just about there and *they want to change
positions on you!* "Let's flip over this way. . . ." *Hey,
wait a minute!* And they change on you before you
even notice it, they just move and I've lost it. So I've
learned that when I hit that peak to tell someone,
"Don't move. Please don't move. It's perfect for me
now." You can say it. Whisper in their ear. Bite their
earlobe. Don't just pray for it, honey—hold 'em by the
ear!

In case you've missed the point, we'll try some other messages: "I need to get my rhythm together—changes throw me
off." "I need only twenty seconds or so, but the longer we keep
the rhythm, the better it is for me." *"Tell* him, 'Keep doing
that.'" "I need steady pressure for up to a couple minutes." "I
need the right position and spot—but then he must stay con-

stant." "I really feel let down—no, it really *ticks me off* if I'm building up and he changes."

Partners should not only take careful note, but *memorize* the above. Nothing is more important than a steady, reliable rhythm as a woman approaches her threshold.

There are some qualifications. A few women prefer a slowly increasing rhythm. Sally, for example: "I want it a little quicker, a little steadier, with very deep penetration." For many women, but certainly not all, the sensations of intercourse, spread within her vagina and broadly upon her clitoris, are sustainable much longer than sensations of cunnilingus. Ginger: "With intercourse, I need a foreplay of two to twenty minutes, then I build a rhythm of maybe forty seconds to a minute or minute and a half. But with oral, I can't keep the final sensations that long—my clitoris gets too sensitive." And, within one woman, this preorgasmic time span can vary from climax to climax—all the better reason for her clear communication. Even then, the moment can come and go, and very often does. Kate: "It doesn't take me long, but now and then I lose it. It's like you're hitting and hitting, and then somehow the motion is just feeling the same. You get numb to it. You lose the friction and rhythm." Caring partners will start again, and slowly rebuild sensation.

## *Approaching . . .*

And now what happens? A woman is within, let us say, some two dozen seconds of climax.

As a woman becomes aroused, and then approaches orgasm, her pelvic arteries dilate, engorging her vessels with blood and swelling her genital tissues. Her clitoris and vestibular bulbs, labia, vagina, and uterus may all congest and expand, transmitting signals to her brain of rising warmth and tension. Her brain, her limbic cortex, activates and coordinates a sense of heightening pleasure. Her pelvic muscles—clitoral, vaginal, PC, and anal—also engorge and innervate with pulses of rising excitement. Neuromuscular tensions may grip her entire body. Her sexual tensions rise and rise until she can barely contain them.

At this moment orgasmic women surely do not back off; orgasmic women *expand* their tensions—until they must erupt. As she approaches her threshold, she centers her physical efforts on those that will boost her across:

I stop concern for my partner. If, for example, I'm fellating him, I might keep on to arouse *myself,* but not give it a thought—I concentrate on myself, my own sensations and feelings.

My most effective position is when I'm on top of my lover. So, coming near climax, I'm so intent on controlling my condition, on getting the angle right, that I might put out a steadying hand and close my eyes or just look away. I'm shutting out all distractions.

When a certain pleasureness is achieved, where I *never* want to lose that sensation, I stay in the same position and maintain that certain motion—and if that sensitive spot starts to fade, I quickly relocate my body.

When I feel it's coming, that I'm going to want or have one, I start a rhythm going by contracting my vaginal muscles—maybe adding assurance. But I try to enjoy that level a while—to increase would mean to climax, and then it would all be over!

I move to rub my pelvic area just the way I want it, or, if I'm in oral, I move to get more intensity, directly upon my clitoris.

During this time, if she can, a woman maintains her sensations just right, sometimes increases intensity, and starts her orgasmic rhythm. Her mind, if she hasn't blended yet, centers on sensation.

Ginger explains, "At the beginning, I'm bonded with him mentally, maybe with thoughts and roles, and I have this way, from outside the bed, of seeing myself making love. But toward the end, my mind is on my skin, my body. I close my eyes and feel myself a part of my sexual feelings—that is all I am, and 'me' is only that. I'm all vagina and clit." Emily, who, throughout making love, mainly dwells on sensations, expresses a similar feeling: "When I'm close to coming, and then when I'm having an orgasm, I feel like a big vagina. Not in a negative sense of course, but celebrating the feminine, something really nice. Your body gives you great pleasure, your body gives you a gift."

Alice, the woman with golden hair who usually has body-part images, states: "I can't always lock the images out, but when I'm getting near the point, I try to turn them off. I see and feel my uterus first, pear-shaped, in rhythmic spasms, but then I'm into sensation alone because that intensifies feeling. I go with what's going on, and images go by the roadside." Nora relates, "Just before orgasm, everything is centered around my genitals. I'm totally aware of that part of my body . . . there's nothing around, I'm not even, sometimes, really aware of my partner." And Lisa: "Moods and visualizations stop—I just don't need them any longer. All my concentration is in my pelvic sensations, and, when you cut away all the crap, that's what it's all about. At that point, when I'm having orgasms, if the phone rings or the house is on fire, it's just too bad, I'm busy. And it's *exhausting*. After it's over I just feel, God, I've used every muscle . . . and drained every emotion."

If she hasn't done so already, these are the moments of letting go, surrendering to nature. "Roles and images go away; I'm lost in sensation." "Once it really starts, my mind switches to physicals." "I build, then switch to sensation, a rush coming out of my body." "My thoughts go to clitoral feelings; I mentally release myself and focus on certain areas." "It's almost like I center, mind blends into body." "I make a final push, concentrate on sensations to get over the mountain." "It all just fades away . . . orgasm takes over." "Relax, let go of consciousness, and totally blend with your partner."

Within the closing seconds, even if she carries an early image through orgasm, a woman's final visions represent her sensations. Wendy, for example, often uses "hot" to describe her pleasurable feelings; at orgasm, she is very aware of bodily heat, and often sees this vision: "I'm surrounded by liquid midnight blue, and magic, floating, silver dots are shimmering on the aura, like sunlight reflecting on water, and I feel flashes of color . . . and then, right as I'm coming, my head and body emerge, and I get the feeling I'm melting, as if from some great fire— an exhilarating feeling that makes me feel strong."

Within these final moments, an image may represent "orgasmic inevitability"; unless the unforeseen occurs, climax will come in seconds. Irene, a sleek, statuesque black woman, married, in her mid-thirties, often has this experience: "I never see this when I'm not going to have an orgasm, and it's short, a second or two. Then it ceases to exist, I don't see anything at orgasm. I'm thinking that this is it, the buildup and then the release, and it's an abstract picture of the sensations I'm feeling. It's in color, but not even real colors . . . more like if you get hit on the head and patterns fleet through your mind. If it were an art piece, I'd probably call it 'Tension.' " And Coral knows her orgasm looms when a body-part image surfaces: "Often, right before orgasm, I feel my labial lips engorge and picture the changing colors, pink, red, purple, and then, at orgasm, bursting. . . ."

To boost herself into orgasm, a woman may also try to recall past, successful sensations. Ros is twenty-one, single, a physical therapist who is quite aware of her body: "I can tell when I'm nearing an orgasm, and the thought of coming close excites me even more. There's different reactions for everyone, but mine are sweaty hands, an increased pulse and heart rate, and tension through my body. . . . If I'm feeling I can't achieve one, I think about past sensations, like what feelings, exactly, made me have one last time. If that doesn't come to me, I'll picture a past encounter, trying to match the image with sensations I was feeling." Or instead, as with Rachel, a woman's mind may always return to tried-and-true stimulations: "Wherever my mind might have been, before I come, when my genitals seem like half of my body, and I'm real, real aware that I'm very, very close, I switch back to the feelings of being especially submissive, that he's making me have these sensations."

One last example. When a woman maintains a fantasy of watching others make love, she makes her final sensations theirs, or empathizes with action and thought, "feeling" their sensations. Or, if she and her partner are both within an image, her final focus shifts to herself and her own preorgasmic sensations. Florence, for example, is forty-eight and divorced, a pretty, amply proportioned woman who teaches art at a college: "I feel transformed and beautiful whenever I'm making love, and I see a mental image of everything going on. And I visualize my sensations, like feeling the friction and contact, and seeing my vague, circular walls closely touching his penis. . . . But then right before orgasm, when I kind of start losing consciousness, I stop my vaginal muscles and transfer to myself. A vivid, romantic image . . . A Judy Chicago painting of flowers might be a way to describe it. Looking down from above, I see an actual penis plunging into a whirlpool. But the whirlpool has the texture of the inside of a flower, multicolored ridges of reds and pinks and blues, a vertical pattern with motion, flowing down to the center, pulling, sucking in. . . . Maybe it lasts some seconds, and then my mind is gone. . . ."

## *Closing In . . .*

We are several seconds away.

An orgasmic woman is active in these, her last, and usually decisive, moments before her orgasm. She does not leave fulfillment to chance. She has built her sexual tensions until her seams are bursting—and now overloads sensation.

Aside from her main sensations, those where attention is focused, half the women need or enjoy another trigger or boost that helps her cross the threshold. Sometimes the boost is mental, like Rachel's switch to submission or Ros's thought that she's close. Thoughts like these may be silent words—"When I start my final rhythm, I tell myself 'Get ready for it, now, now, now . . .'"—which sometimes erupt into sound: "Getting near, I think to myself, 'I can't last any longer,' and cry it out to my husband—'I'm feeling great, I'm getting ready, can't stop, I'm going to come!'" Some women may grow more silent, needing to totally focus themselves on one outstanding sensation, but many others escalate sound in the moments preceding orgasm: "Coming to climax I start to purr like a growing crescendo in music." "It's natural to express myself and moan and scream at orgasm." These sounds and words stimulate, provide communication, and also ventilate pleasure. And a little help from her lover might add a note of excitement—his loving or even dirty word, his audible sounds of enjoyment.

But most final triggers or boosts give more direct stimulation. A lover's kiss is always nice, as is, sometimes, his climax: "When mine is there just waiting, his ejaculation brings my final, complete one." Or a last vaginal pulse: "I usually tighten my muscles, like giving a final push." Nipple or breast stimulation: "Cupping or firmly fondling my breasts . . ." "More intense on my nipples. Teetering there on the edge, an extra press or nip or suck always pushes me over." An anal caress or insertion: "Pressure or touching my anus intensifies the ending." "A finger added deep inside might instantly bring me to climax . . . and also prolong my contractions." Or, perhaps, a combination will push her over the threshold: "Any last-moment sensations can help bring off my climax—and better many than few, so long as he keeps me going at the place where I'm really aroused."

However nice these additions, a partner must be careful to not overdo his caresses. Her primary focus is elsewhere, centered on the sensations that are sweeping her to the threshold, and this is not the moment to cause her undue distraction.

Two or three seconds away . . . A woman not only centers in, but notches up the tensions overcoming her body. Her actions and feelings may well have begun before her steady rhythm, but now they gather momentum, a smooth, unanxious tightening flow, without self-conscious direction:

I both actively do it, and it also just seems to happen. My thighs, legs, vagina, hands—everything totally stiffens. I clench my fists and grit my teeth—so hard I've chipped a tooth.

I'm a clutcher, grabbing him, the bedpost, sheets, and everything gets rigid. My nipples get so sensitive that stimulation must stop there, the skin of my inner thighs feels as if it's rising, and I tighten up my muscles, vaginal, buttocks, and anal . . . until I lose control. . . .

I feel warm and juicy, with little pubic vibrations. My body starts shaking, I grab, tighten my thighs and pelvis, begin to hold my breath. . . . My body goes rigid below my waist and then I'm arching back. . . .

With an oral or manual clitoral orgasm, or when I'm on top in intercourse, I strongly tense my thighs and legs, my vaginal muscles and buttocks. But with a vaginal orgasm, when he's on top or from the rear, I don't tense nearly as much.

My body heat starts to rise, spreading from my clitoris through my breasts and head. I'm consciously slowing down and know I'm tensing everything, PC's, buttocks, arms, and thighs—and sometimes getting a charley horse. Everything gets taut . . . tensing brings my climax.

Several women perceive these tensions as out of their control: "My thighs and legs go straight and split, all my muscles tighten—but it's all involuntary, nothing I 'do,' though all my muscles are hurting. . . ." "I raise my hips, my legs go rigid, my thighs and abdomen tighten, I clench my fists and bite my lip—but it all just occurs, I don't consciously plan it." However, the great majority state that they both create and enlarge, as well as react to tension, and many women consciously tense throughout the moments of orgasm.

In the event that she tenses too soon, a woman may need to "back off." Nora: "I'll start tensing up in order to have an orgasm—tightening up my thighs, my pelvis and my abdomen, pulling in my vaginals, starting a natural rhythm. . . . But sometimes I have to back off or else I'll get cramps in my thighs —it's almost like I'm trying too hard, and I'm not really there yet. So then I'll just relax, then slowly start tensing again."

Finally, many women who consciously tense completely let go at orgasm: "My whole body tautens—and then I just let it flow." "I concentrate on tightening—and then a need to release and explode." And Emily states it best: "I'm tightening every-thing, thighs, vagina, pelvis, arms, getting tense and excited, like racing for the finish line a little out of control . . . and then I just relax throughout the final explosion."

One or two seconds away, cresting the moment of orgasm— and nearly every orgasmic woman gives herself a final lift of overpowering pressure! She overloads sensation, overwhelms her threshold. Whatever her previous motion, she slows herself or *stops,* and presses toward her lover. And a woman usually wants her lover to either keep his rhythm, or to mirror her own actions, to slow or stop and press toward *her.*

*Ingrid:*
I raise myself in intercourse, as well as oral and manual, and he should press, roll in, hold still, press deeper and harder, and not break what's going on— *don't break the connection!*

*Grace:*
I don't want him to stop, but I want more pressure downward, holding firmer and deeper, and I also press my clitoris down, pulling at his buttocks. On top I'm almost more frantic, the feelings seem more clitoral, I'm using my vaginals less, and he'll push up and press, while I bear down for pressure. . . .

*Meredith:*
I prefer to be on top—below, I'll still arch back—and have him keep some movement, though keeping deeper contact, while I press down and arch for vaginal and clitoral pressure. In oral and manual, both of us press —I want clitoral pressure.

*Heather:*
Right before an orgasm, it helps me if my partner presses deeper and harder—and then just holds, stops moving at all, right through my orgasm. I use my own rhythm entirely on top, press my pelvis down and arch, or flatten out on his body, rubbing for clitoral pressure.

*Brenda:*
I usually prefer the bottom, and both of us deeply press at the end, though one out of ten I really want

banging, deeper and harder thrusting. It's clitoral and
vaginal pressing, a deep, deep pelvic feeling, and I want
extreme pressure on my pubis, thighs, buttocks. . . .

*Michelle:*
At the point of orgasm, if a man doesn't know me
well, I have to show what I need. In intercourse, I
clutch, stop and hold him in—grasp him with my legs
—for maybe two or five seconds, until my legs stop
quivering. Manually, I arch myself and grab his wrist
and hold it. Oral is somewhat harder, but I do lift my
hips and softly hold his head, pressing my clitoris
toward him. I try to do it gently, and certainly not
with crudeness—you're in the heat of loving and a
good man wants to please you.

*Rita:*
I want him to continue exactly what he's doing; don't
change horses in midstream. This is working, this is
good, and it's like I could almost take over from here.
When I feel the orgasm approaching, I will say,
"Harder," or "Faster," or "Deeper," or "Stimulate my
clitoris," or "Suck my breast," or something. It's
coming, it's coming, but I've got to work up for it, it's
going to be got at just the right spot and that's how
it's got to be. . . . On top I'll roll my clitoris, arch
back and pull him in, holding clitoral contact, or lift
my hips on the bottom, using my vaginal muscles,
holding him stronger and deeper, or arch and press
with manual and oral—the moment I'm coming I want
something in me, fingers or his penis. . . .

Clearly, a woman's needs at orgasm vary with her source of
arousal. Nora explains, "With oral, if I'm extremely aroused,
a feather touch is enough and right. At other times I need and
want more pressure and stimulation. In intercourse, on the

other hand, I always want deep penetration, and almost press to a stop the moment I'm close to coming. And I do the same for my second—as soon as he starts up again, I raise and stop and come. . . ." Another woman states, "I usually thrust up my pelvis, tense, stop, and hold with both oral and intercourse. But sometimes, in intercourse, we get caught up in the movement, and his thrusting—and our excitement—actually steps up the pressure and prolongs and heightens my climax."

And, during intercourse, a few women usually prefer to keep their movement going, or, on occasion, to increase thrust and motion. Vivian is one: "I hold him closer for contact, using my arms and legs, but I want to keep on moving and I let him take over the rhythm." And Bernadette is another: "With manual I raise and press, manipulate my own body, but in intercourse both of us just go with it, keep the motion going, and sometimes I like to move faster, and deeper for vaginal impact."

Nevertheless, however derived, the concept is almost always the same, a need for final deep pressure to overload her system and enable her to cross her threshold to orgasm. Whether these feelings are vaginal or felt throughout her abdomen, whether primarily clitoral or suffused throughout her vulva, whether several or all, an orgasmic woman needs, and also helps obtain, these final, pulsing moments of overwhelming sensation.

And then, if she hasn't done so already, she surely lets herself go, surrenders herself to nature, gives up all control. . . .

## The Moment

All at once her tensions release, culminate or explode, and a woman knows that her body has reached its sexual peak, a mystic yet mundane experience, fleeing description by words. . . .

*Emily:*
I'm lost within the explosion . . . slow-motion
firecrackers bursting in my pelvis, shooting up my body
and traveling down my legs. I'm lost in a black open
space as if I'm removed from my body, heavy, with no
arms or legs . . . elevated for moments to this nice,
eternal place. . . .

*Julia:*
Unless I stay up for another, I feel a complete release.
My body trembles and jerks, and tingles inside my
vagina run through my body like chills. But then
there's a final, complete one, one that I love but beg
him to stop . . . from vaginal or clitoral or both. The
fire starts in my toes and works all the way up, like
burning, tingling numbness, and just when it's starting
to come alive, I go way over, beyond . . . into the
ultimate experience. . . .

*Rita:*
My body tightens and straightens . . . I feel a surge of
relief. Tiny needles dance through me, and if it's a
vaginal feeling, it moves from my hips on down. A
clitoral starts at my neck and shoulders, rushing
through my body. The good ones seem like fifteen
seconds because it's like a volcano erupting, and
sometimes I see it happen. First the ashes, then the
lava, then the cooling down . . . a volcano goes along
with the feelings in my body. Then I lie some minutes
and let my body cool out . . . enjoying what has
happened.

*Lisa:*
I'm totally out of control . . . and feel it's a sudden
implosion, everything hurling in, converging to my
inside. I'm trembling, gyrating, conscious my nipples

protrude . . . and then in a second it transfers—
sensations in my vagina and pelvis travel up my spinal
cord and flash with light in my head . . . like
someone's massaging my brain, like beautifully going
insane. . . .

*Ingrid:*
My whole body trembles, but I don't feel vaginal
contractions. It's like I go over a hill in a car, and then
my stomach goes flying. I get that free-fall feeling
every single time, until I'm actually gasping . . . it
takes away my breath.

*Heather:*
A rush of incredible feeling . . . like everything ceases
for maybe a second, as if I don't exist. Nothing exists.
And yet I'm aware of pure sensation, my vaginal
muscles contracting . . . and then my breathing comes
back, my heart starts beating again, and all the
sensations flood in. . . . Yet, just for that instant, it's
like I transcend existence. . . .

An infinite number of feelings . . . for every woman it's
different. And different each time she makes love, with each
orgasmic experience.

Her mind subjectively comprehends a moment of special
existence, and her body speaks its joy, differently each time
perhaps, yet nonetheless with conviction. Lubrication seems to
flow, she may experience spasms, tremors, quivers, vibrations
coursing throughout her body. She can feel tremendous vaginal
contractions, or lose them—if she feels them at all—in total
body reactions. She can feel heat or chill, tingling or vibrant
explosions. She can feel a loss of control . . . or simply feel
warmth and comfort. Her body may tense, go rigid, or feel
relieved and tranquil. The moment may leave her soft and
warm, exhausted and drained of energy, or leave her feeling

energized, charged with a need for activity. She may laugh with giddy pleasure, or cry with profound emotion. . . .

Often she feels sensations radiate through her body. "It spreads," "flows out," "it's in my head," "it ends in my fingers and toes." Feelings may start in her clitoris and quickly enfold her vagina, or start with a uterine, vaginal feeling, spread to her clitoris, and swiftly envelop her body. It rushes up, it rushes down, begins "up under my diaphragm," begins "in my breast and glans."

And many women are certain that orgasms vastly differ, not only in their intensity, but also in their "kind." Eve explains, for example: "There are two totally different sensations, a clitoral orgasm and a vaginal orgasm—positively! They're like night and day. For me, a clitoral orgasm is more like a burst of energy that takes my entire body, more of a total release. A vaginal orgasm is more of a total weakness . . . hard to explain. It's more confined and deep, all my muscles contracting, and yet it's all-encompassing—my whole vaginal area is just totally exploding. . . ." For other women, the feelings are rather opposite: "A vaginal climax is stronger, exploding me head to toe. . . . Powerful, deep, leaves me worked out, sinking into the bed . . . A clitoral seems more sharp and intense, but more confined to my vulva." The source of stimulation may also have an effect—whether from oral or intercourse—as does a woman's readiness to have another or more. Several women described two or three "distinct sensations," often vaginal, "G spot," and clitoral. For most of these women, however, the "best" orgasm usually results from a combination or blend of sensations, usually achieved during intercourse.

The women's subjective feeling impressions often have common themes. Fireworks, explosions, volcanic eruptions, heat. Waves of pleasure, waves of water course through her body. The earth trembles beneath her; she soars or falls through space. Her body is taken over; her body is swept away. Electric pulses shock through her; overloads short her out. But joy is *always* her theme, she says, joy and sensual pleasure.

And where is her mind? For the great majority of women, her mind is blank or gone, her existence is pure sensation. Most know nothing but blackness, a few feel whiteness or light. Kristin: "Where is my mind at orgasm? *Gone,* hopefully! My images dissipate. My mind keeps working up to the point where my body takes over more totally—and then there's the heat, the energy, I'm just gone. I swear that's why people enjoy orgasm, because that's the point when they don't exist, the 'little death,' as the French say. I'm sure that's what orgasm is—when the mind is not there."

A substantial minority of women, however, occasionally or consistently, create orgasmic images that represent their feelings. Their images always include, of course, bodily sensations. Fluid may be visualized "cascading through my body," and color comes in waves, or "faster, faster spirals, closing in on sensation." Tamara, who visualizes axons in arousal, sometimes sees this at orgasm: "It starts twenty seconds before . . . almost like a Rorschach test. Intangible moving blots, a pattern of black and white, forming before my eyes . . . It starts slow, builds up, comes down, and then starts working fast—that's when the little ones, endies, start shooting out zip zip." The pace and degree of change in her blots tend to mirror her spasms, tapering to a slighter change with smaller, final contractions.

Grace sees several images, reflecting her moods and sensations: "Sometimes my mind is blank, but I often see a fluffy white cloud, a soft puff of cumulus, and it's usually with a soft orgasm, with gentle, enjoyable feelings. When I'm very dominating, when I leave the primitive jungle cave, I see lion and tiger colors, red-reds, oranges, and greens. I also see stars ignite, or blocks of color like sunrise, or sheets of bursting color, sometimes vivid, sometimes soft . . . a really neat sensation like the glowing northern lights."

One of Natalie's images, although perhaps most common, sometimes reflects, for her, a feeling of great emotion: "Some are quiet and gentle, a flowing release, dissolution. . . . But with that special complete one, I'm into letting it happen, feeling that total explosion. My whole body shudders and I know it sounds so trite, but I see colors and flying sparks, everything like fireworks. . . . Sometimes I cry then, I'm so relieved and delighted. It's like a baptism, regaining my youth, a confirmation I still exist . . . the feelings of being a woman."

And Tracy sees an image, both personal and eternal: "A feel of heat and coming is rushing through my body . . . a surge of relief and pleasure. Beginning a tad before, just before it peaks, I usually have a vision that I've had for many years.

"It is a union, definitely, two becoming one, a union of two spirits. It's very spatial, two dynamic masses of energized color. All the molecules move and they're usually shaped in squares . . . inert, moving gas making different shapes. The shapes come together, touch and overlap, but they never come together where it's only just one mass. The colors in both are alike; orange and purple predominate, then tinges of yellow, varied reds, vivid hues of green. . . . The masses interlap, overlap, or change—as if I turned a kaleidoscope, a constant state of flux —and right when there's my orgasm, the colored shapes explode, travel out with force, so fast they're fading away. They fade away to the side, recede from peripheral vision, as if it's like a bird, wings outstretched . . . to freedom. Up and out, they disappear, and nothing is left in the center. . . . It's all-encompassing, all right there, I've been released to freedom. My spirit is free once again . . . I'm one with the universe."

# 11

# Multiples . . .

After two or three, I stay relaxed and tell myself, "I want more of this feeling."

—*Sonia*

Once she becomes orgasmic, or should she desire to expand or renew her sexuality, a woman may want more than one orgasm during a lovemaking episode.

However, before we take up several or many, let us take up none. Why does an easily orgasmic woman fail to have an orgasm? Although the average woman in this study is orgasmic in over 90 percent of her sexual encounters with a partner, now and then she misses.

Various reasons for not reaching orgasm, usually involving concentration, may be deduced from our previous chapters: severe partner conflicts or shortcomings; the distractions of everyday problems; inadequate time for foreplay or arousal; feeling or being actually sick, or imbibing too much alcohol; a partner who seems not to care, or one who rejects her mood or a favored lovemaking activity. In addition, it may be her first time in bed with a man, causing restraint or awkwardness, or a partner may prematurely ejaculate or not maintain his erection. Or a woman might "just turn off," deciding she's made a mistake in choosing this partner for sex. Another frequent cause is fatigue; at that particular moment, she simply lacks the energy to make the required effort. And the most common reason is that she is "not in the mood," and yet makes love because she cares, to accommodate her partner.

When they are not orgasmic, a few women feel disappointed or remain physically on edge, or need to point a finger of blame, either at themselves with guilt or at an inadequate partner. However, the great majority of women accept the occasional lack of orgasm with absolute equanimity: "I once thought an orgasm was necessary, both for him and to 'prove' myself, but I know it will happen another time, and it's not always important; love and sensuality are fully enjoyable without it." "I *love* to have orgasms, but it doesn't 'have to' happen—if my body does it, it does it. Making love is still fun and closeness, tenderness and warmth. . . ."

And many women, now and then, make love without the least desire for achieving orgasmic pleasure. Love and caring is foremost, the pleasure of being together.

## Bringing on Multiple Orgasm

She has reached an orgasm, and feels submerged in joy and warm erotic sensations. Physically exhausted, emotionally drained, she may have a sense of completion, pleasured enough for the while.

However, she may also feel *more* aroused, and want her sensations again, not in hours, days, or weeks but rather in minutes or seconds. A woman's physiology is such that her deep vasocongestion resolves rather slowly. And, dilated more than at the start, her vascular network may also receive new congestion more easily. It is also possible, depending upon the individual woman and the form of stimulation—whether, for example, clitoral or deeply vaginal—that different reflex pathways are involved in her climax. Her reflex may be "phasic," rapid and susceptible to quick repetition, or perhaps more total and "tonic," or a combination of both. In any event, should stimulation continue and should arousal stay high, many women desire and have more than one orgasmic peak during a lovemaking hour. Some three-quarters of the women in our study, at least on occasion, have had multiple orgasms during a lovemaking session.

Many women experience what might be termed "compounded single orgasms." That is, she may experience more than one orgasm during an extended session, but each is more or less distinct, separated by sufficient time so that prior arousal and tension have substantially resolved. Or a woman may experience "sequential" multiples, fairly close together—roughly from two to ten minutes apart—with little interruption in sexual stimulation or level of arousal. And finally, a third of the women in our study, at least on occasion, experience "serial" multiple orgasms, those separated by seconds, or up to two or three minutes, with no, or barely any, interruption in stimulation or diminishment of arousal. There are, however, no firm boundaries between these "types," and a woman's actual feelings may blend or combine the sensations. Also, within one episode, she may have different types at widely varying times.

What forms of stimulation encourage multiple orgasm?

Most commonly, the women experience two or three sequential orgasms from *changing* stimulation. A usual pattern is one or two orgasms from oral or manual clitoral stimulation, and then, within several minutes, one or two during intercourse. A woman rarely reverses this pattern by having an intercourse orgasm first. A prior, more clitoral orgasm fully arouses her genitals, and seems to ease the way for a later one during intercourse. Further, she may experience her vaginal climax as more "complete" and sating, and of course it may result in her partner's ejaculation. The change of stimulation allows her to stay aroused without undue sensitivity; intercourse spreads her sensations beyond a narrow, repetitive focus.

However, for other women, a constant, concerted focus may be the source of a series of orgasms. Sometimes oral sex will be the source of her multiples:

*Darcie:*

I normally have one and then come down before I get
up for another. But with oral, if he hits and keeps the
right spot, I can have a couple and then hit a stretch
of unrelieved intensity, maybe a minute, one after the
other, until he has to stop . . . until I almost pass out.

*Rita:*

I have the most with oral sex, though not necessarily
the best, and I do like to lie back sometimes and give
myself up to enjoyment. I will be an active partner, but
I also enjoy the feeling that someone is doing to me
and for me. I can have four or five little ones and
maybe a semi-volcano, until a last volcano effect
washes me away. . . . If I rest maybe twenty minutes,
I'll have a second volcano, but I need lots of body
caressing and intercourse when I'm on top.

And other women are most orgasmic during vaginal intercourse:

*Bernadette:*

I seem to have one or two, separated by several
minutes, and sometimes these first are with his hand,
but always inside my vagina. And then if we keep
going, about eighty percent of the time, the next ones
come bang, bang, bang when he penetrates hard and
deep, maybe three or four or more within a couple
minutes, different in intensity but seeming to go up, up,
and the final contraction is strongest.

*Nora:*

With oral, I might have a single orgasm, very intense
where I can't be touched for maybe a minute or two,
or else I might switch from a small one in oral and
come again during intercourse, within ten or fifteen
seconds. But usually they come in intercourse, sort of

grouped in a "series," like two-three-four, ten seconds
apart, up and down in intensity, and then a pause of a
minute or two and then another series. . . . I normally
have one or two of these groups, but if it goes three or
four, I can't take any more.

For several women, like Kate, multiples come from a combination of vaginal and clitoral sensations: "I can have one in
oral, with lots of body stimulation, and then another quickly by
changing to vaginal sensations. My vaginal sensations build,
and changing positions can bring on another, minutes or seconds apart—but I know that I need a total sensation . . . my
body, my breasts, my clitoris, his penis hitting the side of my
walls, touching the edge of my lips . . . a total combination of
several stimulations."

What can a woman actively do to help bring about her multiples?

For several women, the advent of multiple orgasm is
thoroughly unpredictable: "Somehow everything seems to be
'right.'" "I know how to hold them off, but I never know in
advance how or when they'll happen." A few women mention
their moods: "I can't really predict my moods, but they affect
my level of excitement." "I don't think I do things differently,
but I guess it depends on how sexy I feel, more my moods and
emotions." For others, the crucial element is her partner, who
continues pleasurable stimulation or "has enough stamina" to
bring her to another. A lover's "enthusiasm" helps, and one
woman states that her husband "decides" whether or not she
will "go for it": "He seems to sense how hot I am, and makes
me want to have more."

However, half the women take active steps to enhance the
probabilities of obtaining multiple orgasm. For some women,
the crucial factor is her attitude: "I learned through masturbation, and now I know it can happen—I know I can still maintain a level of high arousal." "Once my body and mind accepted
it, that my body can accommodate several, there was no prob-

lem at all. But I never think of multiples as something I 'ought to' have—that can make me have none."

After an orgasm, though all women swiftly or eventually return to centering on sensation, she might also add an image to help maintain her arousal. Alice, the woman with long blond hair, uses body-part images, and Lily envisions a flower: "I visualize on the sensation, and it always seems or feels like a flower opening up. I visualize my vagina, my whole vulval area, as growing open and swelling. My mind may wander, but to reach multiple orgasm, my mind comes back to that. I have to concentrate on myself, and I feel the flower get bigger and bigger . . . until I'm just a 'center,' and opening, burgeoning petals. . . ." And Peg, who always has many orgasms, states that her first is "more physical, but after that they're more mental. Then I'm more relaxed and I visualize more what I feel. We continue stimulation, and thoughts come back by themselves— fantasies or mind's-eye pictures of what we're actually doing, or seeing his touch in oral love, or seeing him in me in inter- course. But I'm concentrating on feeling, and everything fades at an orgasm. . . ."

As previously noted, a woman might consciously choose to maintain a particular sexual position, or continue a specific stimulation, or consciously change sensations. She also may feel that it's crucial to simply "keep on going": "I keep him in rhythm by holding his buttocks, and keep my own body going." "Keep your effort, keep your arousal, keep those sensations flowing. . . ." And finally, although once she hits her stride, a woman often relaxes and gives herself up to the sensation, most women help bring one or two more by keeping tension and pressure: "I tighten my vaginal walls to bring myself up for more." "It's a conscious decision as to whether I'm going for more than one, and it works about nine out of ten. I tighten and tense my whole body, and hold a pitch of tension throughout my entire climax. Then I'm still up for more . . . relaxing eases excitement." "It's tension and pressure. During orgasm, I press up to my partner and trigger more contractions, and then to continue momentum, I go to a vaginal tensing rhythm and always keep some pressure, my clitoris pressed to his pubis. . . ."

And, of course, to bring about multiple orgasm, several propitious factors are usually working in concert. A woman may be in her sexiest mood and feel a very strong physical need to have another orgasm; her partner may be affectionate, the emotional climate caring; her lover may love her pleasure, and also know what turns her on, her favorite source of sensation; she may have learned to tense or relax, to bring herself up for another; and she may employ an image, her most erotic visions. . . .

## Ultra-Orgasmic Women

Four women, Julia, Vivian, Peg, and Sonia, are so extremely orgasmic that we have termed them "ultra-orgasmic."

Sonia, married, is in her mid-thirties, from a Methodist family background. Lissome and attractive, she projects a gentle manner; her work is handling customer complaints at a local department store chain. During lovemaking, Sonia sometimes has fantasies—"like someone who is gentle, saying nice things" —and always has third-person images: "It's like a mirror; I'm aroused by seeing what we're doing at the time, but I concentrate on the feelings." Her primary mental arousal, however, comes from going with moods: "My husband gets the idea, but I can change if his mood is stronger. Sometimes my mood is sweet and I want him to teach me all over again, and I'm always on the bottom for this. Or else I can be a nice little girl but still a mischievous tease. On top I'm more aggressive and do more of the loving, and sometimes I feel submissive and want him to take me. . . .

"Just before reaching orgasm, my mind is all in my body. I usually have about ten and they seem to come in a series or group. Like I can have two or three with oral, ten to thirty seconds apart, and then switch to intercourse and go right on having them, about ten in four or five minutes, and they seem to build in intensity . . . until my final big one, where I feel like he has to keep going. I arch or press down against him and grab or pull him to me, his body, head, or hand, and my body starts shaking, my feet get hot, and it feels like a soft explosion; my whole insides are quivering, exploding over the hill. . . . Then, if I want them, if I rest for five or ten minutes, I can start another group. . . ."

Sonia has never wished to "test" her orgasmic capacity; she usually has about ten, and often has up to thirty. Julia has six to a dozen, and has counted over one hundred. Vivian becomes "most sensitive after three or four," usually has "ten or twelve," with twenty in an hour "common," but has never bothered with an "upper count," feeling it rather irrelevant. Peg, on average, has "twenty to thirty," and her husband has counted "close to one hundred."

Aside from impressive numbers and, one must assume, generally "conducive" physiology, these women have little in common. For example, only two women, Vivian and Peg, describe a vaginal area of particular sensitivity; even then, they do not obtain most orgasms from stimulation of the area. Neither Julia nor Sonia ever actively or consciously use their circumvaginal muscles. Before multiples, Julia always tenses her body and seeks an extreme of pressure, Peg sometimes does, Vivian rarely tenses but usually seeks added pressure, and Sonia only seeks pressure when having her "final, big one." Three women, Julia, Peg, and Sonia, extensively use a form or forms of erotic mental arousal; Vivian mainly blends her mind with felt erotic sensations. . . . The ways in which they differ continue on and on.

These women do share one characteristic, however, which also is often mentioned by other multiply orgasmic women—the placing of *trust* in their partners. They and their partners know and value their great orgasmic capacity, and the women utterly abandon themselves to pleasure, sensation, and love-making.

Three of the women are married, and Vivian, with "so much, complete faith" in John, has lived with him for two years. Julia, we know, "surrenders" herself, often helpless in bondage. Sonia says, "With each orgasm I get more relaxed, and want more, and go with it. My theory on why I'm orgasmic is I want to make us both happy. I like the feeling and I trust my husband. Why would I want to hold back?" And Peg relates, "I have to feel that no matter how orgasmic I am, no matter what I do, he's still going to be around. You have to trust a man, and then completely let go."

In terms of becoming orgasmic, the real issue, the heart of the matter, goes a step beyond trust. After all, many nonorgasmic women completely trust their lovers or mates, and other women are very orgasmic with men barely worthy of trust. But within an aura of trust, a woman is much more able to give up all control—and *that* is the heart of the matter, of value to any woman. Eventually Peg and Sonia get to the crucial point: "Why would I want to hold back?" ". . . and then completely let go."

And so these women bring us full circle, back to the "golden rule." No matter with whom, when or where, to get even *one* orgasm, a woman must let herself go.

And let us not forget that "more" does not necessarily mean "better." Meredith, who often has multiple orgasms, speaks for many women when she states her feelings this way: "They usually start during intercourse, and probably when I'm on top. When I've already had an orgasm, it doesn't take much more to maintain that level of high. Sometimes it takes nothing, all he has to do is to keep the stimulation. I can have, easily, three at once, and if we kept on going . . . I really don't know how many. Because I don't care and I don't like it that way. It gets too intense, almost bordering pain, and it takes the head off pleasure. I like a little space. And so, if there's three, I like a

nice relaxing one and one that's big and explosive, and I like
to slow it down enough to really feel each. And one can be
enough—pleasure isn't in numbers."

We conclude this chapter with Michelle's account of her
feelings during multiple orgasm. She is always multiply orgasmic, usually serially, and like many orgasmic women, she often
feels "pulsations," or a feeling of "suspension," before she has
an orgasm.

"When I'm really on a high plane, I feel like I have a throbbing sensation. . . . This sensation fills up, and it seems like it
gets harder and harder and harder. Then all of a sudden—I
don't know whether I'm doing it, trying to stop it, or whether
my body's going and I have no control—it seems there'll be
little hesitations in the pulsating, it'll stop, it's not as rhythmic
as it was. Like I'm really up and feeling good, ready to reach
the peak, and something is going: 'Stop, not yet, not yet, not
yet.' It's involuntary, God knows I want to get there, and it's
only intensifying feelings, making me more eager. . . .

"I feel like I'm getting taut all over. My whole sensation is
breasts and nipples and vaginal walls. I almost feel like my
breasts are growing, like they're filling up and I'm just . . . I'm
so alive and I'm getting ready to erupt, just boom! I feel I could
swallow the whole world up. It feels like I want to take everything inside me. I feel like I'm indestructible, the greatest,
biggest, and best. I feel that nothing, at that particular moment,
not a thing in the world could harm me, hurt me, touch me in
any way. I'm right there and alive.

"My body tremors all over at orgasm, I feel it deep in my
vagina, my outer lips. My vagina clamps and pulsates, I bear
down, and sometimes see flashes of light—yellow, green, red.
Then I seem to relax, and the clamping slowly eases. . . .

"I become very relaxed once I have my first orgasm. And I
*let myself go.* I focus on what I've just experienced, the feelings,
and then I find myself building up again because the feeling was

so terrific and I enjoyed it so much, and of course my partner is continually working with me, keeping the constant pattern going. He doesn't even have to be touching my body. He can move to my ears and my neck, kissing me, my eyelids, it all just keeps on going. It's a very low, relaxed feeling, and then if he continues to kiss and caress and touch, I start going up again. . . . Sometimes it takes a while, sometimes I get there quite fast. . . ."

# 12

# And Afterglows

After we've made love, it's almost like a first kiss . . . or like we seem one body, feeling each other's sensations. A bond between us, a warm feeling in the atmosphere . . .

*—Ginger*

You have shared a beautiful joy.

After making sexual love, bodily tensions slowly resolve. Sex seems incomplete without some shared affection, or quiet moments of love. . . .

An afterglow of making love may last for hours or days. Later that day or before you sleep, or possibly the next morning, you may rerun an image of the lovemaking in your mind.

Perhaps your perceptions will change. "After I've had an orgasm, it takes a while to emerge from that. All my perceptions become more abstract, the world becomes more ethereal, I see more meaning and essence. . . ."

Or, perhaps, you will quietly sleep, drifting off in reverie:

"Half asleep, between dreaming and waking, my mind slips off in dreams. . . . I see two people, alone, within a romantic setting, perhaps within a cabin deep inside a woods, or possibly on an island of black, volcanic sands. . . . They are going to sleep together, the type of people we are. . . . The two of us."

## *As We Part . . .*

Each woman in this study is an individual. She varies in our basic parameters—age, race, marital status, and family religious background. She varies in educational attainment, occupation, affluence, whether or not she has children; her life may have been untroubled, or she may have overcome obstacles. She has a single orgasm, or ranges up to two dozen, during an average encounter. Her physical attributes vary, from her genital and sexual endowments to her weight and shape, the color of her eyes, the hue and cut of her hair. She is whimsical or pensive, assertive or cautious, exuberant or shy. During lovemaking, she has one or another physical preference, and her mind solely centers on sensation or is moved by mood or emotion or is filled with a sensual stream of lovely erotic images. She is unique. And yet she is just like you. . . .

Through all these differences, a cohesive portrait of an easily orgasmic woman emerges. She has gained a good measure of personal independence, has formed her own sexual identity; she takes an active part in obtaining sexual pleasure; she makes her own sexual decisions. She has come to know her sexual self, has explored her own body and sexual responses, has learned her personal needs and desires, her own sexual style. She starts on warm by preparing herself for coming sexual encounters. During lovemaking, she eliminates distraction and concentrates on pleasure. She communicates with her partner, in some manner informing him of her personal tastes and desires, her state of growing arousal. She seeks the stimulations that normally bring her to orgasm, and orchestrates a totality of mounting physical sensation. She is mentally sensitive to her favorite erotic stimuli, and lets her mood, her preference, take her mind where it wills. She approaches orgasm by seeking and centering on steady stimulation, enlarges her physical feelings, and soars across the summit with an overload of sensations. She builds, creates, and, however she might do it, she obtains enough stimulation to cross the threshold of orgasm. And always, always, she *lets herself go,* surrenders herself to nature.

As our conversations ended, as we parted, we asked each woman's opinion on the one essential factor in becoming more easily orgasmic. Their responses can be distilled to three themes.

The first essential, the keystone, is getting to know yourself, delving into the mysteries that make you an individual, learning your secret thoughts and desires, your body's idiosyncrasies; learning about your reactions, how your body and mind respond to growing arousal and feeling, how you prefer to help create a surplus of total sensation. And then you must *accept yourself* without reservation or guilt, love the wonders discovered, appreciate your gifts.

The second theme speaks of your sexual relationship. Accept only a caring partner, or sensitize a loved one to your personal needs and desires. And then you must reveal yourself, share and explore with someone you trust, and above all *communicate,* before, during, and after sex, to truly commune with a partner.

And lastly, the women expressed a theme of care and affirmation:

You can get to that marvelous peak of sexual feeling. Believe you can do it. No matter what it takes, you are going to get there. You are capable. Every woman is capable.

Your mental attitude is first, a positive feeling for pleasure, a positive feeling for sex. Sex has to be good —people have been doing it since the beginning of time, and not just for procreation. It is meant to be for personal joy, and sharing love with a partner.

You are capable of having pleasure, of being orgasmic. Let it flow. Don't hold back. Don't hold back. . . .

* * *

And so you and we must part, with a word of gentle counsel. Feeling anxious twinges about your sexual "performance" (Will I be "good"? Reach orgasm?), or feeling self-conscious during lovemaking, or being hyperaware of anything you are doing—all these will only destroy your chances for sexual pleasure. Read, File, and Forget. Read or glance through this book again, perhaps now and then refer to it, now and then experiment with something you have read about, but as you are making love, forget this information. In time it will be second nature, if it is not already. Immerse yourself in the instant, enjoy your precious moments of sensual sexual love, exalt in being together, sharing a moment of joy.

The essence of the women you have met is that they have found the freedom to use their natural gifts.

Be patient. Nature will be kind to you. Give Her your mind and body. She will give you ultimate pleasure.

# APPENDIX A

## *Interview and Research Method*

By design, we obtained 75 percent of our participants through the personal contacts and recommendations of interview assistants and other women interested in the study. The remaining 25 percent were obtained through advertising, primarily in general circulation periodicals. A nominal fee was paid for each interview, and the average woman invested between four and five hours of her time. Prior to each interview, the women were sent a summary description of the research project, a pre-interview questionnaire, and an acknowledgment that stated they were at least twenty-one years of age, understood the subject matter of our interview, and understood that they could discontinue the interview at any time they wished (no woman ever desired to do so).

Participants were carefully screened at several stages for reliability and their proper inclusion in the group (sixty-four interviews were conducted to obtain the final sixty). First, women were screened through conversation with the researchers; those who, by general impression, did not meet the criteria (which included psychological stability) were dissuaded from participation. The women were then given a vague criterion for inclusion in the study, that they be "easily orgasmic," to ensure that our minimum criterion of 75 percent not be parroted back to us. The questionnaire, and other pre-interview screening forms used later in the study, asked a direct question on the subject; women who fell short of the criterion, or who were vague or inconsistent in their answers, were given careful and polite reasons—none involving their orgasmic capacity—as to why we could not proceed with the interview.

We made every effort to not "predetermine" the results of the study; therefore, no participant was eliminated because her answers failed to "fit" preconceptions. However, because of our parameters for a demographic distribution, we were not able to interview all qualified and interested prospective participants. (Also, unfortunately, we were not able to "name" all sixty women appearing in the book.)

All interviews were conducted by a male/female co-interview team. This proved an effective method for obtaining comprehensive and reliable data. The presence of both a male and female defused the situation of any threatening (sexual) overtones, and allowed the participant to choose, if she wished, which sex she more easily related to. Further, one interviewer was able to carefully listen while the other conversed, thereby picking up stray threads and inconsistencies.

Before every interview, we prepared an "analysis" of each woman's questionnaire; both interviewers had copies. Although the interview format was informal, free-form, and exploratory, and we encouraged each woman to dwell at length upon the areas which *she* thought important, the questionnaire analysis allowed us to always cover certain key areas, as well as areas of special interest to the particular woman, as indicated by her questionnaire responses. Every interview was tape-recorded.

The team approach also allowed two opinions as to a woman's reliability, particularly on the subject of her orgasmic consistency. During the interview, several—or many—questions were asked on the subject, and after the interview, both interviewers consulted about a woman's reliability as to this particular question and her general reliability. When the interviewers had substantial doubts about this or another key area, the interview was eliminated from the study.

Although this book is addressed to a general audience, we attempted to use a careful scientific method throughout the study. We have compiled any number of numbers—for example, women from a Protestant religious background were orgasmic during an average 91.106 percent of their encounters and a median of 92.9167 percent; Catholic, 90.01 percent average and 92.5 percent median; Jewish, 90.7416 percent average, 90.0 percent median. Women in the age group 21 to 29 report an average of 2.85 orgasms per encounter; 30 to 39 years, an average of 2.91667; 40 and older, 3.3 orgasms—yet each age group reports a median of two orgasms per encounter. Fifty-six women report a total of 625 separate visual images during sexual encounters. . . . And so on. . . . Yet because the study did not proceed from null hypotheses, or measure occurrences against contrasting or control groups, we have not seen fit to present numbers such as these.

We were conservative in evaluating all responses, and were particularly cautious in evaluating responses concerning a G spot, vaginal sensitivity, and ejaculation. All humans are vulnerable to suggestion as to how they should function sexually —and women feel under constant pressure to "have what they're supposed to have and do what they're supposed to do." A funny thing happened on the way to completing our interviews: *The G Spot* was published, and suddenly G spots were mentioned with somewhat greater frequency. Any area of vaginal sensitivity was liable to be labeled a G spot. One woman (her interview was eliminated from the study) had little vaginal sensitivity at the beginning of our interview, and then developed a G spot midway through. We do hope our book will dispel some of this need. The vast majority of women in this study do not have a sexually functional G spot or a particularly large clitoris or hair-trigger breast sensitivity—or any form of special sexual equipment or reactivity. *No* woman (assuming she has no irreparable physiological dysfunction) needs more than her natural self to be easily orgasmic.

We also hope that researchers, therapists, and other health professionals will find our work to be of value.

# APPENDIX B

## PRE-INTERVIEW QUESTIONNAIRE ON FEMALE ORGASM

WE WOULD APPRECIATE YOUR GIVING A BRIEF EXPLANATION FOR ALL QUESTIONS (NOT MERELY A SIMPLE YES OR NO), BUT WE'LL CERTAINLY UNDERSTAND IF YOU SKIP ONE OR TWO. IF MORE SPACE IS NEEDED FOR AN ANSWER, FEEL FREE TO CONTINUE ON THE BACK OF THESE PAGES. TRY TO PLACE YOURSELF IN THIS CONTEXT: A DEAR FRIEND OR CLOSE SISTER ASKS YOUR HELP. . . . SHE HAS A REASONABLY DESIRABLE PARTNER BUT HAS DIFFICULTY ACHIEVING ORGASM. WHAT DETAILED AND SPECIFIC ADVICE CAN YOU GIVE HER?

## PERSONAL BACKGROUND:

1. HOW OLD ARE YOU? _____

2. MARITAL STATUS: (CHECK LINE)
   LIVING WITH YOUR LOVER ......................... ____
   MARRIED ........................................ ____
   SINGLE AND LIVING ALONE OR WITH A PLATONIC ROOM-
   MATE .......................................... ____
   SEPARATED ...................................... ____
   DIVORCED ....................................... ____
   WIDOWED ........................................ ____

3. IF APPLICABLE, HOW LONG HAVE YOU BEEN MARRIED OR LIVING WITH YOUR LOVER? _____

4. EDUCATION COMPLETED:
   ELEMENTARY SCHOOL OR LESS ..................... ____
   SOME HIGH SCHOOL .............................. ____
   HIGH-SCHOOL GRADUATE .......................... ____
   SOME COLLEGE .................................. ____
   SOME GRADUATE SCHOOL OR MORE ................. ____

5. FAMILY RELIGIOUS BACKGROUND _____
   OCCUPATION _____

6. AT WHAT AGE DID YOU FIRST HAVE SEXUAL INTERCOURSE WITH
   A MAN? _____

7. HOW OLD WERE YOU WHEN YOU FIRST HAD AN ORGASM AS PART
   OF SEXUAL INTERCOURSE (EVEN THOUGH IT MAY HAVE BEEN AS-
   SISTED BY OTHER STIMULATION)? _____

8. DO YOU HAVE ORGASMS EASILY IN MOST SITUATIONS? _____

9. ARE YOU EASILY ORGASMIC WITH PRIMARILY ONE PARTNER OR
   CAN YOU BE SO WITH SEVERAL? _____
   WITH A PARTNER YOU'VE ONLY KNOWN BRIEFLY? _____

10. HOW OFTEN DO YOU HAVE SOME FORM OF LOVEMAKING SEXUAL
    EPISODE _____ AND WHAT
    PERCENTAGE OF THE TIME DO YOU REACH ORGASM? _____

11. HAVE YOU LEARNED TO BECOME MORE ORGASMIC OVER TIME?
    _____
    DID A PARTICULAR PARTNER HELP YOU LEARN? _____

12. DO YOU FEEL YOU SHARE (OR HAVE PRIMARY) RESPONSIBILITY
    FOR OBTAINING ORGASM, OR IS IT YOUR PARTNER'S RESPONSIBIL-
    ITY? _____

## MENTAL AND PSYCHOLOGICAL ASPECTS:

13. WHEN MAKING LOVE, DO YOU TRY TO AROUSE YOURSELF MEN-
    TALLY? _____ DO YOU TRY
    TO ESTABLISH A PREFERRED MOOD, "ROLE," OR EMOTION? ___
    _____

14. WHEN MAKING LOVE, IS THERE A TIME WHEN YOU MAINTAIN MEN-
    TAL CONCENTRATION ON PHYSICAL SENSATION? _____
    _____
    ANY SPECIFIC SENSATIONS? _____

15. AT SOME STAGE APPROACHING ORGASM, DO YOU FOCUS YOUR
    MIND ON SPECIFIC BODY PARTS (SUCH AS YOUR CLITORIS, LABIA,

VAGINA, ETC.), OR AREAS (YOUR VULVA, PELVIS, ETC.) TO THE EXCLUSION OF MOST OTHER THOUGHTS? _____

_____

16. IS IT IMPORTANT TO LET YOUR PARTNER KNOW WHAT STIMULATION YOU WANT? _____ AND IF SO, HOW DO YOU COMMUNICATE YOUR PREFERENCES? (VERBALLY? YOUR BODY POSITION? MOVING HIM/HER? MOANS, ETC.? OTHER?) _____

_____

17. DO YOU EVER FANTASIZE WHILE MAKING LOVE? _____

_____

18. HAVE YOU EVER HAD A BISEXUAL ENCOUNTER OF ANY KIND? __

_____

19. DO YOU EVER USE ANY POPULAR DRUGS, ALCOHOL, X-MOVIES, OR EROTIC PARAPHERNALIA OR DRESS TO ENHANCE SEXUAL AROUSAL? _____

_____

20. WHILE MAKING LOVE, DO YOU SOMETIMES THINK OF YOURSELF IN A SPECIAL WAY (SUCH AS SWEET, BAD, DOMINEERING, DESERVING OF PUNISHMENT, ETC.)? _____

_____

WHICH WAY(S) OF FEELING ABOUT YOURSELF BEST ASSISTS YOU IN ACHIEVING ORGASM? _____

_____

21. IS THERE ANYTHING UNUSUAL OR "QUIRKY"—THAT YOU THINK YOU ALONE MIGHT DO—THAT HELPS YOU OBTAIN ORGASM? (IT MIGHT NOT BE AS UNUSUAL AS YOU THINK/FEAR, AND BE OF HELP TO SOMEONE): _____

_____

## PHYSICAL STIMULATION AND BODY ASPECTS:

22. HOW IMPORTANT IS YOUR GENERAL PHYSICAL CONDITION TO YOUR ABILITY TO ORGASM EASILY? _____

23. DO YOU ACTIVELY USE YOUR VAGINAL (PUBOCOCCYGEAL) MUS-
CLES DURING INTERCOURSE? _____

24. DO YOU RELATE ANY OF YOUR ORGASMIC ABILITY TO YOUR PAST
OR PRESENT MASTURBATION? _____
_____

25. IS YOUR FAVORED STIMULATION OR BODY POSITION IN MASTURBA-
TION SIMILAR TO THAT WHICH BEST HELPS YOU OBTAIN ORGASM
WITH A PARTNER? _____

26. WHAT TYPE OF PHYSICAL STIMULATION MOST OFTEN HELPS YOU
TO ORGASM (E.G., INTERCOURSE, ORAL, MANUAL, OR ANAL STIMU-
LATION OR ANY OTHER)? _____
_____

ARE ANY COMBINATIONS OF THESE MOST EFFECTIVE? _____
_____

27. TO OBTAIN ORGASM, IS A SPECIFIC STIMULATION ALWAYS (OR
OFTEN) NECESSARY TO YOU? _____
_____

28. WHAT INTERCOURSE POSITION(S) IS MOST EFFECTIVE IN HELPING
YOU OBTAIN ORGASM? _____

29. CAN ORAL SEX BRING YOU TO ORGASM? _____
MANUAL SEX? _____ ARE THESE EVER MORE SATISFAC-
TORY THAN INTERCOURSE? _____

30. IS THERE A PARTICULAR SENSATION YOU FEEL (THAT YOU COULD
ADVISE ANOTHER WOMAN TO STRIVE FOR) THAT YOU KNOW WILL
LEAD TO ORGASM? _____
_____

31. HOW DOES YOUR BODY REACT AT THE PEAK OF ORGASM? _____
_____
_____

WHAT DOES ORGASM FEEL LIKE? _____
_____
_____

32. DO YOU EVER MAKE A CONSCIOUS DECISION TO "GO FOR OR-

GASM," AND THEN FEEL IT'S RIGHT TO USE YOUR PARTNER'S BODY
AT THAT TIME TO OBTAIN IT? _____
_____

33. IF YOU ARE HAVING DIFFICULTY BECOMING AROUSED, IS THERE
ANY "MOST OFTEN SUREFIRE" STIMULATION YOU SEEK THAT USU-
ALLY IS ABLE TO TURN YOU ON? _____
_____

34. HAVE YOU EVER HAD "MULTIPLE" OR "SEQUENTIAL" ORGASMS
(TWO OR MORE IN A ROW WITH SECONDS OR MINUTES BETWEEN
THEM)? _____
_____

THANK YOU! PLEASE RETURN YOUR UNSIGNED QUESTIONNAIRE AND
SIGNED/DATED ACKNOWLEDGMENT; WE WILL THEN SCHEDULE AN IN-
TERVIEW.

# SELECTED BIBLIOGRAPHY

*Chapters 1 and 2*

Appleton, William S. *Fathers & Daughters.* New York: Berkley
Books, 1984.

Barbach, Lonnie Garfield. *For Yourself: The Fulfillment of Female
Sexuality.* New York: Doubleday & Co., 1975.

Crenshaw, Theresa Larsen. *Bedside Manners.* New York:
McGraw-Hill, 1983.

de Bruijn, Gerda. "From Masturbation to Orgasm With a Partner:
How Some Women Bridge the Gap—and Why Others Don't."
*Journal of Sex and Marital Therapy* (1982):8:2:151–167.

Dodson, Betty. *Selflove and Orgasm.* New York: Betty Dodson,
1983.

Fisher, Seymour. *The Female Orgasm.* New York: Basic Books,
1973.

Friday, Nancy. *My Mother/My Self.* New York: Dell Publishing,
1977.

Halpern, Howard M. *Cutting Loose: An Adult Guide to Coming to
Terms With Your Parents.* New York: Bantam Books, 1978.

Heiman, J., LoPiccolo, L., and LoPiccolo, J. *Becoming Orgasmic:
A Sexual Growth Program for Women.* Englewood Cliffs, N.J.:
Prentice-Hall, 1976.

Hinton, Ann P., Sherby, Linda B., and Tenbusch, Lynne G.
*Getting Free: Women and Psychotherapy.* New York: Grove
Press, 1982.

Kaplan, Helen Singer. *The New Sex Therapy.* New York:
Brunner/Mazel–New York Times Book Co., 1974.

Kassorla, Irene. *Nice Girls Do.* Los Angeles: Stratford Press, 1980.

Kline-Graber, Georgia, and Graber, Benjamin. *Woman's Orgasm: A Guide to Sexual Satisfaction.* New York: Fawcett Popular Library, 1975.

Margolies, Eva L. *Sensual Pleasure: A Woman's Guide.* New York: Avon Books, 1981.

Masters, William H., and Johnson, Virginia E. *Human Sexual Inadequacy.* Boston: Little, Brown, 1970.

Weis, David L. "Affective Reactions of Women to Their Initial Experience of Coitus." *Journal of Sex Research* (1983): 19:3:209–237.

Westheimer, Ruth. *Dr. Ruth's Guide to Good Sex.* New York: Warner Books, 1983.

## Chapter 3

Byrne, Donn. "The Imagery of Sex," in *Handbook of Sexology,* J. Money and H. Musaph, eds. Elsevier/North–Holland Biomedical Press, 1977.

Research supporting the view that fantasy during sexual relations is commonplace and normal:

Harriton, Barbara E., and Singer, Jerome L. "Women's Fantasies During Sexual Intercourse." *Journal of Consulting and Clinical Psychology* 42(1974):3:313–322.

Sue, David. "Erotic Fantasies of College Students During Coitus." *The Journal of Sex Research* 15(1979):4:299–305.

Talbot, R. M. R., Breech, H. R., and Vaughan, M. "A Normative Appraisal of Erotic Fantasies in Women." *British Journal of Social and Clinical Psychology* (1980):19:81–83.

Research on physiological response to internal and external mental erotic stimulation:

Heiman, Julia R. "A Psychophysiological Exploration of Sexual Arousal Patterns in Females and Males." *Psychophysiology* (1978):14:266–274.

Hoon, Emily F. "Biofeedback-Assisted Sexual Arousal in Females." *Biofeedback and Self-Regulation* (1980):5:2:175–191.

Stock, Wendy E., and Geer, James H. "A Study of Fantasy-Based Sexual Arousal in Women." *Archives of Sexual Behavior* (1982): 11:1:33–47.

## Chapters 4 and 5

Bandler, Leslie Cameron. *They Lived Happily Ever After.* Cupertino, Calif.: Meta Publications, 1978.

Barbach, Lonnie. *Pleasures: Women Write Erotica.* New York: Doubleday, 1984.

Kinsey, A. C., Pomeroy, W. B., Martin, C. E., and Gebhard, P. H. *Sexual Behavior in the Human Female.* New York: Pocket Books, 1965.

Mosher, Donald L. "Three Dimensions of Depth of Involvement in Human Sexual Response." *Journal of Sex Research* (1980): 16:1:1–42.

## Chapters 6 and 7

Comfort, Alex. *The Joy of Sex.* New York: Crown, 1972.

Comfort, Alex. *More Joy.* New York: Crown, 1974.

Hite, Shere. *The Hite Report.* New York: Macmillan, 1976.

Langone, John. "AIDS: Special Report." *Discover* (December 1985):28–53.

*Sexuality Today Newsletter.* " 'Sexual Alignment' Techniques." June 4, 1984.

## Chapter 8

Masters, William H., and Johnson, Virginia E. *Human Sexual Response.* Boston: Little, Brown, 1966.

The G Spot, vaginal sensitivity, and female ejaculation:

Alzate, Heli. "Vaginal Eroticism and Female Orgasm: A Current Appraisal." *Journal of Sex & Marital Therapy* (1985): 11:4:271–284.

Belzer, E. G., Whipple, B., and Moger, W. "On Female Ejaculation." *Journal of Sex Research* (1984):20:4:403–406.

Goldberg, D. C., Whipple, B., Fishkin, R. E., Waxman, H., Fink, P. J., and Weisberg, M. "The Grafenberg Spot and Female Ejaculation: A Review of Initial Hypotheses." *Journal of Sex & Marital Therapy* (1983):9:1:27–37.

Heath, Desmond. "Adversaria: An Investigation Into the Origins of a Copious Vaginal Discharge During Intercourse: 'Enough to Wet the Bed'—That 'Is Not Urine.' " *Journal of Sex Research* (1984):20:2:194–210.

Hoch, Zwi. "Letter to the Editor: The G Spot." *Journal of Sex & Marital Therapy* (1983):9:2:166–167.

Ladas, Alice Kahn, Whipple, Beverly, and Perry, John D. *The G Spot.* New York: Holt, Rinehart and Winston, 1982.

Perry, John D. "Letter to the Editor: G Spot Co-Author Replies to Hoch and Alzate." *Journal of Sex & Marital Therapy* (1984):10:2:142–144.

Several books cited elsewhere in this bibliography (e.g., *The G Spot, For Yourself,* and *Becoming Orgasmic*) have excellent sections concerning use of the circumvaginal muscles. Also see:

Britton, Bryce. *The Love Muscle.* New York: New American Library, 1982.

Chambless, D. L., Stern, T., Sultan, F. E., Williams, A. J., Goldstein, A. J., Lineberger, M. H., Lifshitz, J. L., and Kelly, L. "The Pubococcygens and Female Orgasm: A Correlational Study With Normal Subjects." *Archives of Sexual Behavior* (1982):11:6:479–490.

Freese, M. P., and Levitt, E. E. "Relationships Among Intravaginal Pressure, Orgasmic Function, Parity Factors, and

Urinary Leakage." *Archives of Sexual Behavior*
(1984):13:3:261–268.

Messe, M. R., and Geer, J. H. "Voluntary Vaginal Musculature
Contractions as an Enhancer of Sexual Arousal." *Archives of
Sexual Behavior* (1985):14:1:13–28.

Genital compatibility:

Fisher, W. A., Branscombe, N. R., and Lemery, C. R. "The
Bigger the Better? Arousal and Attributional Responses to
Erotic Stimuli That Depict Different Size Penises." *Journal of
Sex Research* (1983):19:4:377–396.

Vatsyayana. *Kama Sutra.* New York: Castle Books, 1963.

## Chapter 9

Abrahamson, D. J., Barlow, D. H., Beck, J. G., Sakheim, D. K.,
and Kelly, J. P. "The Effects of Attentional Focus and Partner
Responsiveness on Sexual Responding: Replication and
Extension." *Archives of Sexual Behavior* (1985):14:4:361–371.

Douglas, Nik, and Slinger, Penny. *Sexual Secrets.* New York:
Destiny Books, 1979.

Friday, Nancy. *My Secret Garden: Women's Sexual Fantasies.*
New York: Pocket Books, 1974.

Gawain, Shakti. *Creative Visualization.* New York: Bantam Books,
1982.

Maslow, Abraham H. *Motivation and Personality.* New York:
Harper & Row, 1954.

Singer, Jerome L., and Switzer, Ellen. *Mind-Play: The Creative
Uses of Fantasy.* Englewood Cliffs, N.J.: Prentice-Hall, 1980.

## Chapters 10, 11, and 12

Amberson, Ingrid J., and Hoon, Peter W. "Hemodynamics of
Sequential Orgasm." *Archives of Sexual Behavior*
(1985):14:4:351–360.

Bohlen, J. G., Held, J. P., Sanderson, M. O., and Ahlgren, A. "The Female Orgasm: Pelvic Contractions." *Archives of Sexual Behavior* (1982):11:5:367–386.

Bohlen, J. G., Held, J. P., Sanderson, M. O., and Boyer, C. M. "Development of a Woman's Multiple Orgasm Pattern: A Research Case Report." *Journal of Sex Research* (1982):18:2:130–145.

Bridges, C. F., Critelli, J. W., and Loos, V. E. "Hypnotic Susceptibility, Inhibitory Control, and Orgasmic Consistency." *Archives of Sexual Behavior* (1985):14:4:373–376.

Gallagher, Winifred. "The Etiology of Orgasm." *Discover* (February 1986):51–59.

Graber, Benjamin. "Circumvaginal Musculature and Female Sexual Function: The Past, Present and Future." *Journal of Sex & Marital Therapy* (1981):7:1:31–36.

Levin, R. J. "The Female Orgasm—A Current Appraisal." *Journal of Psychosomatic Research* (1981):25:2:119–133.

Sherfey, Mary Jane. *The Nature and Evolution of Female Sexuality.* New York: Vintage Books, 1973.